Crossroads

Choosing

Your

Tomorrows

Today

Crossroads

Choosing
Your
Tomorrows
Today

Charlene Bell, Ed.D.

Sunburst Publishing
A Division of American Corporate Advisors, Inc.
520 S. Pierce • Suite 224
Mason City, IA 50401
Phone 515-424-3187

CROSSROADS
Choosing Your Tomorrows Today
Copyright © 1990 Charlene Bell

Library of Congress No. 89-051433
    ISBN 0-9624320-0-8

The author gratefully acknowledges permission to quote from the following:

"The Station" from **A Penny's Worth of Minced Ham: Another Look at the Great Depression** by Robert J. Hastings, © 1986 by the Board of Trustees, Southern Illinois University.

"The Man Who Thinks He Can" by Walter D. Wintle from **Poems That Live Forever** selected by Hazel Felleman. (New York: Doubleday and Company, 1965), pg. 310.

"Hanging In There" **There is Nothing I Wouldn't Do if You Would Be My POSSLQ (Person of Opposite Sex Sharing Living Quarters)**, Charles Osgood, (New York: Henry Holt, Inc., 1981), p. 27-28.

Somewhere A Master: Further Hasidic Portraits and Legends, Elie Wiesel, (New York: Summit Books, 1982), p. 173

First Edition, First Printing
Printed in the United States of America

Published by SUNBURST PUBLISHING
Suite 224 * 520 S. Pierce
Mason City, IA 50401

ABOUT THE AUTHOR

Dr. Charlene Bell is a psychologist, educator, consultant and speaker. She has published numerous articles in newspapers and association journals in addition to presenting seminars to business and professional groups nationally and internationally. She has been on the teaching faculties of several major state universities and presently owns her own consulting firm.

For Claudia, Steve, and Larry . . .

. . . my best teachers . . .

You taught me how to love.

TABLE OF CONTENTS

ACKNOWLEDGEMENTS

To Lorna Bell, without whom this manuscript would not or could not have been written. In addition to her professional expertise, I am blessed with her patience and her love.

To Arlyn Miller, for his support and his continued professional assistance.

To my mentors - Virginia Lewis, who started me on my journey, and Lucille Knox, who has persevered in teaching an often unwilling and resistant student the knowledge necessary to continue the journey.

To Mike Scott, for his assistance and belief that this message should and could be written.

To Reverend Bill Hines, for his continued inspiration and the sharing of his knowledge.

To Jim Collison, without whose belief and support this message would not have been written.

The Station[1]

Tucked away in our subconscious minds is an idyllic vision in which we see ourselves on a long journey that spans an entire continent. We're traveling by train and, from the windows, we drink in the passing scenes of cars on nearby highways, of children waving at crossings, of cattle grazing in distant pastures, of smoke pouring from power plants, of row upon row of cotton and corn and wheat, of flatlands and valleys, of city skylines and village halls.

But uppermost in our minds is our final destination — for at a certain hour and on a given day, our train will finally pull into the station with bells ringing, flags waving, and bands playing. And once that day comes, so many wonderful dreams will come true. So restlessly, we pace the aisles and count the miles, peering ahead, waiting, waiting, waiting for the station.

"Yes, when we reach the station, that will be it!" we promise ourselves. "When we're eighteen...win that promotion...put the last kid through college...buy that 450 SL Mercedes Benz...pay off the mortgage...have a nest egg for retirement."

From that day on we will all live happily ever after.

Sooner or later, however, we must realize there is no station in this life, no one earthly place to arrive at once and for all. The journey is the joy. The station is an illusion —

it constantly outdistances us. Yesterday's a memory, tomorrow's a dream. Yesterday belongs to history, tomorrow belongs to God. Yesterday's a fading sunset, tomorrow's a faint sunrise. Only today is there light enough to love and live.

So gently close the door on yesterday and throw the key away. It isn't the burdens of today that drive men mad, but rather the regret over yesterday and the fear of tomorrow.

"Relish the moment" is a good motto, especially when coupled with Psalm 118:24, "This is the day which the Lord hath made; we will rejoice and be glad in it."

So stop pacing the aisles and counting the miles. Instead, swim more rivers, climb more mountains, kiss more babies, count more stars. Laugh more and cry less. Go barefoot oftener. Eat more ice cream. Ride more merry-go-rounds. Watch more sunsets. Life must be lived as we go along.

(1) Dr. Robert J. Hastings, **The Station,"** *A Penny's Worth of Minced Ham* (Carbondale, IL: Southern Illinois University Press).

Preface

Once Upon a Time

Most fairy tales begin with "Once upon a time" and end with "they lived happily ever after." As women, we were led to believe that if we were good and kind we would be discovered and rescued by handsome knights on white horses. Our heroes would whisk us off into the sunset to live a carefree and blissfully enchanted existence.

My story — which is certainly not a fairy tale — begins, "I was out to lunch until the age of 30!" And there is no end to my story...just learning ever after.

I reached a point in my life — after having done all of the shoulds, ought to's, and the have to's — when I discovered that there really was no knight on a white horse. There was no one else to assume the responsibility for my life. No one could and no one would. I chose to become my own knight and the horse, as well. I would be the rescuer and the means of escape. I made some difficult choices and, with those decisions behind me, I started on my journey.

I headed out of town in my modern day covered wagon, an old Pontiac with a battered and faded orange U-Haul behind it. I drove off into the sunset with my three pioneering children, greatly enjoying this departure from the ordinary. Little did we know what adventures the future held for this fractured family of venturesome souls.

It was a hot, humid, dusty, windy Nebraska summer day when we set out, with all our worldly possessions in tow, to see the world. Our plan was for me to go to college in preparation for making a living for the kids and myself. I honestly felt like a pioneer as I headed west with minimal resources, minimal support from others, and an abundance of faith and belief that it could be done!

We unloaded our whole lives into a cracker box, two-room apartment provided for married student housing at my chosen college. This was to be our home for the next three and a half years. With borrowed money in hand, I ventured forth to the registrar's office to enroll in my course work. My plan was to become a teacher.

I quickly discovered what it meant to juggle classes, handle children, and manage crises that erupted each day. A good night's sleep was four hours long and a real treat. However, we made it!

The best time to risk is when you have nothing to lose. Again, with borrowed money in hand, I extended my lease and headed off to class to pursue a master's degree. My plan was still to become a teacher, just a more qualified one.

Upon completion of that program, I was asked to join the faculty. The following year, I reassessed the situation and made the choice to continue on for a doctoral degree. I felt that more doors would be opened and more opportunities would be made available to me. I'd also be able to better provide for my family.

Once again, it was time to repack my covered wagon and move on to a new university campus. I had made arrangements for us to live in a trailer. Once again, it was a blistering hot and humid day when we pulled into town. With classes due to begin the following Monday, we were anxious to get settled in our new home.

We were greeted with the happy news that there was no trailer! It would not arrive for several weeks, in fact. There we were — three tired and hungry children and one tired and hungry, fit-to-be-tied mother — with no place to go.

As I sat in the car, I tried to think of any person from this town I might have met, however briefly, or known in the past. Perhaps even a friend of a friend who might live in this community. A name came to me from out of the blue.

I checked the local phone book and, lo and behold, there it was! A woman answered the phone when I called. She listened to the tale of woe that quickly followed my explanation of who I was and how she might remember me best. I had met her husband, a college professor, years ago.

When I asked if she knew of any place we could stay temporarily, she said that all she could offer us was her lightless basement. It sounded like the Hilton to me.

Traveling in style, we had two whole bunk bed mattresses to make this basement our home. The basement floor was cold beneath our feet as we went about setting up housekeeping. In this dim and dreary basement suite, only fragments of our pioneering spirit remained intact.

Somehow, the four of us managed to survive until the last day of summer school when our trailer arrived! (I know, I know. Trailers are no longer called trailers; they are "mobile homes," right? Well, this was a trailer!)

During that summer, I would get up before the sun did. The children, bless their hearts, somehow managed to sleep. I drove to the banks of the Missouri River and waited for the sun to get up so I could study by its brightening light.

We ate our makeshift meals outdoors, generally in the park. All activity ended a bit after sundown. There's not a whole lot a mother can do in the dark with three kids. Of course, there's not a whole lot three kids can do in the dark either when they know their mother's right there.

At the end of August, when we moved to our "palatial" residence, we felt we had finally made it!

Three years later, with my degree in hand, we set off again to our Promised Land! I had chosen not to accept a teaching contract offered at the University of Minnesota. I wanted to follow a different route and obtain field experience as a school psychologist. I wasn't about to fulfill the saying that "those that can't, teach!"

Once again, we packed our covered wagon and set out. Since I couldn't find housing in the city of my employment, we ended up living in a smaller community about 10 miles away.

Once again, we had no money and no place to go. As we pulled into town, I stopped at an intersection...and so did my covered wagon. My trusted Pontiac died a dignified death with its mission accomplished. It seemed to say, "I've brought you this far. I can go no further."

Several businesses, among them a bank, were within view of that intersection. I ran to the bank, introduced myself to a kindly fellow and said: "I have a job. I have no car and no place to live. Can I get a loan?" Thankfully, he okayed my application for a loan and we were immediately able to acquire a newer mode of transportation.

Through the years, I continue to thank and appreciate the trust that banker had exhibited in his dealings with this "damsel in distress."

All this resort community could offer us for our first year accommodations was a rustic cabin with one small furnace. Of course, wouldn't you know, that winter was the coldest one in many, many years. We could have handled the frozen pipes, but when our rugs froze to the floor as well, we feared for our very survival! We sat huddled around the small, little furnace and managed to make it through the winter!

Over the years, this community proved to be supportive and very good to us all. To make a better living during those years, I taught summer school at a university one hundred miles away. I drove that distance twice each day in order to be home with the children.

I began to feel that it was time for a new challenge. I gave up my university teaching, my administrative duties and made the choice to open a private practice. With children in college, my resources were minimal. However, there still was that abundance of faith that this could be done. It was!

After three years of a successful private practice, I felt that it was time for yet another new challenge. Additionally, I could see that I needed to be closer to a major airport so that my public speaking schedule could be better managed and expanded.

I closed the private practice, packed up and sold my home. I headed off in a newer version of the old covered wagon, just knowing it was the right thing to do.

As I pulled into the new city, the weather was no less

accommodating than it had ever been. This time, it was a cold and blustery winter day. Once again, I literally had no place to live. I had minimal resources, but a great deal of support and the same ever-abundant faith and belief in what I was choosing to do. I had no place to live and I had no office. I had no income and no real business. But I still knew the move was right. It was!

Everything finally fell into place. I did, however, live in and out of my car for several weeks until the apartment of my choice became available to me.

It has been an exciting and exhilarating journey, thus far! It has been a challenging journey and, at times, a difficult one.

There were the usual number of broken bones, infections, hospitalizations, cut fingers, emergency room visits, growing-up problems, concussions and convulsions. In addition, there were all the broken down cars, bills that had to be paid, and certainly the added challenge of our living conditions! We made it.

There were good times, too. I think of all the friendships and bonds that were forged throughout this journey. Those we met while going to school. The fun times we had in that two-room student housing apartment and then again in our little trailer! The laughter and the tears as we all struggled with common goals and common problems. Getting our degrees and raising our children topped our lists. There were good times, personally, as I watched my three children all receive their college degrees and get their lives under way personally and professionally.

Looking back over my journey, I believe it can be categorized in this way.

1. **Choices**. We are never without choices. No choice is still a choice. All choices have consequences.

2. **Challenges**. They are the natural result of each and every one of our choices. It is through our challenges that we are stretched to the point where we discover inner strengths and resources. One of the greatest challenges of all is to manage oneself and maximize those resources.

3. **Conquests**. For every challenge there is a conquest. Every conquest is new knowledge. Whether it's through a victory or a mistake in our own thinking, it's all knowledge.

This book is about those choices, challenges and conquests that determine the quality of each individual life. Learning to sort out those areas that are within your control from those that are not is an important lesson to learn.

What follows are some of the management tools that may help you along your journey as you become increasingly able to exert your control. These tools will assist you in the management of your Mind, your Self-Worth, your Emotions, and your Physical Well-Being, as well as in the completion of your Mission.

Hopefully, these tools will make your ride a little less bumpy and a little more joyous. We are all on our own individual journeys and no matter where you are at this point on yours, it is all right to be there! It is never too late to take a risk with your life and to move on in some dimension. No one can make the journey for you. You must make it within yourself, by yourself. Are you ready?

Chapter One

Making The Choice, Living The Challenge

"The unexamined life is not worth living."

Socrates

Life is learning. Life is a journey through a series of multi-faceted classrooms in what I call the "University of Earth."

Coming from our different environments, we each enter this university with the diverse genetic programming that results in our unique talents and interests.

For as long as we exist, we will be students and active participants in a curriculum especially designed to promote growth and personal development. There is no "final" graduation from the University of Earth.

A Lifetime's Journey

All growth is gradual. Learning moves along a kind of endless continuum. Someone once said that it is a man's privilege to live "always learning, but never knowing." We aspire toward ideals and individual goals, but often discover that life is teaching us something entirely different along the way!

A baby falls down many times before it is finally able to stand and walk alone. An athlete suffers many setbacks and defeats on the way to the Olympics. A pianist bores us to tears with tedious practice exercises as he or she prepares for a recital.

Growth is gradual. Mistakes are a necessary evil in our struggle to grow and learn. We learn little by little. We learn because of what we have learned in the past. Learning is a cumulative thing. One revelation comes forth and builds upon those that have come before. Those mysteries of life that have previously escaped us are suddenly unveiled.

2

For example, bacteria have always existed on earth. But scientists were not able to develop cures for bacterial diseases until they **learned** of the existence of bacteria. After learning of their existence, they had to **learn** the properties of the various bacteria and their effects on the human body.

When these secrets were revealed, scientists then were able to develop countermeasures. These revelations triggered the discovery of viruses, and so forth.

George Washington Carver's discovery of the hidden secrets of the peanut is another excellent example of the continuum of learning.

No doubt there are a great many concepts that we, in our present state of unfoldment, are unable to perceive. Learning is a step-by-step process. Sometimes it's hard, though, to measure progress when the forward movement is slow and labored.

We must be careful not to look at life in a rear view mirror. The past is over and done with. However, sometimes reflection is a positive affirmation of how much has been learned and how much growth has taken place. Generally, I find myself exclaiming: "I thought I understood it all back then [maybe just six months previous!], but I have new insights now. I have grown."

Secrets are secrets only for as long as they are unrevealed. We should approach the University of Earth with eagerness and expectation. The higher your vision, the more you see. The greater your knowledge, the more you absorb.

Untapped Potential

We are going to graduate only once from this university. When we do, about 90% of our human talents, capabilities, and potential will remain undiscovered and untapped. We are told that we use perhaps 10 to 12% of our potential. It can even be said that the average person only uses 4, 5, or 6%!

This means that we have endless amounts of learning and discovering to do while on this journey. We can not afford to stand still. We are meant to continue moving and evolving in rhythm with a life that is always going forward and extending itself.

Each of us was created to become infinitely more than what we are right now. Each of us is far more than we think we are. What you are now is never permanent. It is impossible to remain static or fixed because there exists in each of us a spirit that seeks to be more.

Use it Or Lose It

We were not created to sit still or stop growing. As we find it possible to let go and to open ourselves to the creative challenges and rhythms of life, our "potentialities" begin to blossom and we are raised beyond our "actualities."

It is nothing to brag about when we declare "this is the way I've always been and I'll never be able to change."

Let's remember the wisdom of ancient eastern sages. These individuals understood that the person who is consciously evolving is a person who is directing himself

4

toward an unlimited goal. He is not in competition with anyone but himself. He knows there is nothing noble about being superior to someone else and that true nobility is being superior to one's previous self.

Many athletes attempt to follow this sage advice in their training efforts. One day's personal performance is compared to another day's performance in terms of the sport being measured. Time, distance, or whatever have no other meaning than as comparisons to personal goals and previous performances.

Competing against yourself is the surest way to become a winner! Musicians have no other criteria but their own best performance. They might attempt to compare their capabilities to an ideal, but as Mozart once said, "Perfection is a goal and man is allowed to pursue it, never to attain it."

No Snap Courses

Some courses at this university are especially difficult. These tougher classes are the ones that greatly increase our knowledge. The lessons or tasks that came easily to us in the past were the ones we devoted less time and effort to, weren't they? If we don't learn, we are doomed to repeat the course.

Some courses are chosen deliberately. Others intrude and seem not to fit the path we have chosen. The question we should ask is not, "Why did I take this course?" but rather, "What can or did I learn?" Then we can move on along the new path and find another secret revealed. It's not whether we succeed or fail that's important, it's whether or not we have learned anything. Problems are only opportunities for additional knowledge.

There have been many courses in my personal journey that I've had to go through more than once! When I've found myself facing the same obstacles or trials again and again, I find it necessary to stand back and reflect.

I ask myself just what there is about my own consciousness (all that which precedes my experiences) that continues to attract these same situations or individuals over and over again. Once I've gained that knowledge, then I can move on. No longer will that particular situation or person hinder my learning in quite the same way again. (For our purposes, consciousness is defined as **the total of all our thoughts, feelings, and behaviors.**)

I learned in daily private practice over the years to cease asking **why** an individual took a particular course. I found that the question "Why?" forced many individuals to defend their actions in order to protect themselves.

To ask "Why?" forces us to go back in the past and to try to recall the reasons for doing certain things. Because much of our behavior is subconscious, rather than conscious, I found that individuals were making up very creative reasons for being just where they were in their lives.

Instead of "Why?" I learned to ask them **what they'd learned, what they are presently learning, or what they needed to learn to move on.**

Teacher and Student

We all are students and teachers at this University of

Earth. Everyone who crosses our paths will be one or the other or both. There is an old eastern philosophy that says whenever a student is ready, a teacher always appears.

This has certainly been true in my life. Whenever I have reached a point when I've been ready to learn something new, a situation has presented itself or a special person has entered my life. As a result, the particular situation or person served to direct me toward the next level of learning.

I have been blessed in my life not only to have had teachers who instructed me well, but to have had several who were mentors. Occasionally, one is blessed with an individual whose wisdom appears to far exceed the level at which most people function. A mentor must be willing to share his wisdom and to instruct you along your way.

Sometimes we choose our own curricula. That is, we sit down and map out a plan for our lives. We predetermine where we would like to go and what we would like to do. Few people sit down, however, with a plan of how they would like to grow. It would appear that most individuals are not able to outline a future growth pattern because there is too much yet to be discovered and experienced. New opportunities for growth present themselves and proceed to take us on a joy ride of sorts. Frequently considered obstacles to growth and learning, these opportunities seem to throw us off track and cause us to lose sight of where we were headed.

With our limited ability to judge and discern, these side trips appear to have very little sense to them. In reflecting back upon many of these detours, we often find that what we learned brought us back to our paths and that we were never really off course at all.

There is an order to the universe. There is an order in the development of every human being. Babies certainly don't jump before they crawl. Likewise, there is an order in the life of each human being with respect to his development and evolution as a student of learning.

Never Off Course

Perhaps it is safe to say that in spite of our numerous "side trips," we are never out of sync with the order of our unfoldment as human beings.

We are all on this journey. It only makes sense that each of us appears a little off base at times, perhaps even a bit irrational. How could it be otherwise when we aren't finished yet? Our processes are dynamic and unfolding — never finished — in our earthly development.

Sometimes, this becomes a hindrance to the successful exploration of our talents as we begin to compare and to compete with others. The greater your understanding of your many selves, the more clearly you see that you do have the potential to conquer all things that appear before you.

Life forbids settling in or becoming too comfortable. As we look at the lives of the greats, we see that almost all of them instinctively avoided too much comfort. They realized the need for certain basic securities such as food, clothing and shelter so that mind and brain might function effectively. Beyond this, they did not allow themselves to "settle in" or to live too safely or unchallenged.

We must remember that the great field of labor is ourselves. Our first task is the weeding out of old and harmful growths that would only strangle our fragile seeds. Digging in deep and planting those seeds follows this weeding process. Pruning and cutting back our delicate plants helps us to bring forth the fruit of our efforts.

No one can take our tests for us. If we choose to cheat, we will ultimately be forced to go full circle — right back to face what needs to be faced — so that we can grow and move on.

I gave a high school graduation talk recently. It's always a challenging opportunity to speak to high school seniors. They are at a point in their lives when they aren't really open to any "pearly bits of wisdom!"

Undaunted, I forged ahead anyway. I told the class that there was only one thing I hoped would be remembered. I wanted each of them to absolutely savor this particular moment in their lives. There would never be another time when they felt as smart, as sophisticated, and as ready for the challenge of life as they did at this very moment.

I wanted to caution them that this feeling would be repeated, no doubt, on many other occasions throughout their journey. When they left these schoolrooms, they would enter others, not just college classrooms but the schoolrooms of life. Every time they learned a bit of new knowledge or had a new insight, their consciousness would be changed and there would be another graduation.

When each of us struggles through what I call the "biochemistry courses of life," it's not unlike it was when we were really in a school classroom. We find ourselves overwhelmed and wanting to run away. Somehow, we stick it out. When we complete the course and look back, we feel good about ourselves.

We even feel a grudging respect for the teacher who, at the time we were taking the course, we probably thought very little of. However, in reflecting back, we become aware that the teacher believed in us, knowing we could learn. Most importantly, this instructor enabled us to respect ourselves for persevering and learning. Now we are ready to move on.

In our educational experiences, I'm certain we have all discovered that we perform at different levels of competence in different areas of knowledge. The same is true for the five portions of our being. For instance, we might be in college level courses physically and mentally. But sometimes we find ourselves functioning at a fourth grade level emotionally and socially. Spiritually, we might still be in kindergarten!

Ideally, our goal should be to raise the level of our competence within the emotional, social, and spiritual realms, or whichever areas reflect our own personal deficits. However, we need to realize that it is okay to be just where we are. Taking stock occasionally and assessing our progress are major steps in this ongoing process of growth and development.

While we are struggling through the tough courses of life, there certainly is a tendency to admire (and even to envy a bit) those who appear to major in "Recess", taking none but the easiest courses.

However, I do not believe it is possible to make it through this university without, at one time or another, drawing upon our own resources to achieve a goal or to overcome an obstacle.

Getting Unstuck

However, this doesn't mean we won't try to get ourselves "unstuck" when we inevitably find ourselves in difficult courses. There are three popular options we consider when we're stuck.

It seems to be human nature that all of us start with the first option and, wouldn't you know, it's the only option that really doesn't work. That doesn't mean we don't all attempt to fix our lives by charging ahead in this direction anyway.

Pointing a Finger

OPTION 1 - "If it is to be, then I'll change you."

The first thing most of us do is to point our fingers and attempt to blame someone else for causing us to be in our troublesome situations.

We are great finger-pointers. But it's important to remember that when you point a finger at another person, three point back at you! I believe this is just about the right ratio!

I've often said that I don't believe anyone has ever married who didn't think his or her mate could use some changing! Once home, people think it won't take long to change their partners in some way. Most of us point our fingers and try to change others so they will not become an obstacle in our lives.

I would imagine that all who are reading this have at least one person in their life whom they are trying to change.

When we try to change others to better fulfill our expectations, we deny these people their own true natures. Each of us — so unique and never-to-be-duplicated — spends countless hours and energy getting others to be more like us. But we're not even finished products ourselves!

Not only do some people try to change at least one other person, there are those who try to change a whole group of individuals to be just like themselves. While we don't need everyone to be on exactly the same path doing the same things at the same time, I do think there are things we can do to impact the lives of others.

Seeing is Believing

One of the most powerful teaching tools to affect another person's behavior is to model that behavior in such a way that the student sees the benefits of following the example set.

We are great students of observation, far more so than of verbalization. Yet most of us spend the greater part of our time **talking** when our lives and the way they're lived are the best teaching tools.

It's not what we **say** that others evaluate to determine if they want to follow on our paths. It's the **behaviors we exhibit** and the **examples we set** that are judged.

When I practiced as a marriage counselor, it was fascinating to see how often one mate demanded behavioral changes from the other even though he or she wasn't demonstrating this same behavior. I would hear one demand of the other that he or she be loved. I would often ask the person who made the demand if he or she were a loving person. Long silences usually followed this question.

It is true that when we are loving, we are loved. Conversely, when we are hostile, we are treated with indifference. It works both ways!

There is another careful assessment to make when we attempt to change other people's behaviors. We need to determine the payoffs or rewards that are received from the particular behaviors we want to change.

Built in Rewards

Each of us does what we do because our behaviors have built-in rewards. In other words, our behaviors make sense. When someone asks us to give them up — and we don't replace them with better habits — we give up something that provides us with a measure of security and comfort.

If we do give them up, we create a vacuum. And nature abhors a vacuum. Oftentimes, what replaces the original behavior is even worse than what we did in the first place.

I used to ask people to take pieces of paper and draw a line down the center. On the left side, they were to list the pay-offs of a particular behavior being considered. On the right side, they would indicate the price tag for giving it up. (See diagram on page 14.)

We would often take a common behavior or habit, such

as smoking. We listed all of what the individual felt were the benefits, the rewards and the payoffs for smoking.

On the other side of the paper, should they choose to become non-smokers, we listed what it would cost them...what price they needed to pay.

Habit - Smoking	
Payoff	Price Tag
Keeps weight off	Will gain weight
Relaxes me	More stress
Keeps me sane	More insanity
Hands busy	No pockets
Show jewelry	Can't brag
Attention	Ignored
Paid to quit	No reward
Solve problem of unwanted relationships	Smelly breath and clothing
People don't know	Deceit

It became very clear that in order to be willing to pay the price, we needed a third column that would give us a new reward, a better reward, a more fulfilling reward than the original. (See next illustration.)

Payoff	Price Tag	New Reward
		Better health
		Tastebuds return
		Fresh breath
		Make choices
		Love myself
		Empowerment
		No blaming
		Odor-free clothes
		Honesty

We all want something for our efforts and we do want it to be better than what we have.

Oftentimes, we try to change others, especially children, through fear or threat of punishment. I can assure you that any behavioral change based on fear is no change at all. There is one rule of behavior that can be counted on 100% of the time: The more you nag another person to change, the more you ensure he stays the same.

We are "experts" at looking at others and, without knowing, deciding just what it is they need for their growth and development. Perhaps someday we will evolve to a point where we can allow others to be themselves and we will love them anyway. Then we will have arrived at a point where we can be in harmony with others and live with them in a loving way.

I've often said that an indicator of a good marriage is when each party realized that he or she could not (and chose not to) change the other person. One of my clients finally reached this point when she said to herself: "I give up! I'm just going to love my husband the way he is." After many years of trying to change him, it was her change of attitude that turned their marriage around. She was finally able to accept what he could give...rather than focusing on all the things that, in her perception, he could not give.

This option of pointing a finger to find the culprit for why our lives are not going well does not work.

Changing the World

OPTION 2 - "If it is to be, then I'll change the circumstances."

The second choice we have to get our lives on track and move on is to change the environment or the situation that we find ourselves in.

I believe there is some validity in this option. There are times to make career changes or to move in some way. In fact, a short time ago I heard an expert in the field of business say that any college graduate who hasn't changed jobs within three years of graduation will probably not get anywhere.

I found this a startling remark. But then I realized that

there is indeed a time to move and to change for our own growth and well-being. It was not an unrealistic comment, particularly in an age when most graduates will be re-trained at least four times during their working careers. There is also a time, I believe, when it's appropriate to end a relationship. This is particularly evident when it would be self-destructive to remain in the relationship.

It's important, however, that we assess what we've learned from these relationships so we can avoid making the same choices again. If we don't learn, it's likely we'll find a similar relationship and end up in the same situation as before.

Beware the Dangers

The danger in changing environments or changing rela-tionships is that we tend to seek a perfection that is just not there. For instance, there will never be a perfect place to work because unfinished, irregular people work there. (Before you become a little self-righteous, just remember that you're probably someone else's thorn and are perhaps causing him or her discomfort in the work place.)

Above all, there will never be a perfect relationship. We just don't have perfect people yet. Moving from place to place, we chase after perfection. But in spite of all our movings, we still get up in the morning, look in the mirror and guess who moved with us? Perhaps we need to say to ourselves each day when we look in the mirror: "You made me this way. I hope you're satisfied."

I interviewed a man a while ago. He had seven positions

listed on his resume within a rather short period of time. This, in itself, is not all that unusual in this day and age.

When we discussed each of the job situations, I did not ask him why he quit or why he left. (Again, this question makes people defensive. It forces them to make things up.) Instead, I asked him what he learned about himself in each of those seven situations.

... Red Flags

He repeatedly used two words that I call "red flags." I hope these two words don't come out of your mouth too often. They are a dead giveaway for where you are with your ability to take charge of your own life.

The two words he spoke in reference to every one of those jobs were **"if only . . ."**

"If only" his boss had understood him better, he would have made it in one of them.

"If only" the hours had been better, he could have made it in another.

"If only" he had lived closer to work, he would have made it in another.

The "if only-ers" of life become some of our greatest complainers, gripers and groaners. They feel that they are victims rather than active participants in the things that happen to them along their journeys.

Take a look at the following list of "if only's." Place a check beside any that apply or have applied to you in the past:

_____ IF ONLY people would accept me as I am.

_____ IF ONLY I could find friends who didn't have problems.

_____ IF ONLY I had more time to meet people.

_____ IF ONLY I weren't so shy.

_____ IF ONLY I were more handsome/pretty, I'd be more lovable.

_____ IF ONLY I finished college, I wouldn't feel so inferior.

_____ IF ONLY other people were as open and honest as I am, then I could trust them.

_____ IF ONLY I could find someone to depend on.

_____ IF ONLY I hadn't ruined that last relationship. It was probably the best thing that ever happened to me.

_____ IF ONLY people weren't so critical.

____ IF ONLY the world weren't so corrupt.

____ IF ONLY I had more money.

____ IF ONLY I could lose weight.

____ IF ONLY I had different parents.

____ IF ONLY people were nicer and more sensitive.

____ IF ONLY I could begin to change my life.

____ IF ONLY SOMEBODY ELSE WOULD COME ALONG AND STRAIGHTEN MY LIFE OUT FOR ME.

____ TOTAL (If you've checked even one, take another look in the mirror.)

There are people who go all the way through this University of Earth, pointing fingers at others and "if only-ing" their lives away.

Getting to the Promised Land

One of my favorite stories about what happens to complainers is from the Bible. God called Moses to lead the Israelites out of slavery in Egypt to their Promised Land. I believe Moses is symbolic of what happens to all of us when

20

we are given ideas and desires that spur us on to greater and greater things.

Anyway, if you remember the story, Moses answered: "Not me, for I stutter. You wouldn't expect me—who can't speak well — to accomplish such a feat." God answered with reassurances that He would provide all the support and resources Moses needed. Moses obeyed and did free the Israelites from their bondage.

When given inspiration or direction, we too feel that it is impossible for us to do whatever needs to be done. In fact, if some desire or idea appears impossible to achieve, it's probably knowledge coming through you — from the Source of all — telling you there are great things in store.

The most interesting thing to me about this story is, first of all, how ecstatic we are when we are freed from the bondage of any habit.

However, we find very quickly that until we replace the old habit with a new one — or get to that Promised Land — we have to go through a desert. It's well known that it took the Israelites forty years to reach their Promised Land and to actually be freed from slavery. It could also be said that it took forty years to get slavery out of the Israelites. Until they could replace their habit of bondage with something else, they were bound to wander the desert.

I have travelled to Egypt and visited that desert. It would certainly not be a thrilling place to trudge across! I have read, however, that it should have or could have taken a mere eleven days for the Israelites to get from their Egyptian bondage to their Promised Land. Using your mathematical powers, you can quickly figure that they travelled five miles a year — or about seventy feet a day —

and thus stretched their suffering to forty years.

The reason it took them so long was they complained the whole way. They complained about the food. God promised them plenty of food. But as with any group of people, there are always those who do not appreciate the food. These complainers want their food well-done or perhaps they want a totally different cuisine.

They complained, too, about the water. Above all, they complained about the leadership. People without vision often wish to return to slavery. They find it more comfortable to remain slaves of misery than to forge ahead into the unknown.

This was certainly true of the Israelites. And when they finally approached the Promised Land, God could only find two people positive enough to send on ahead.

This story has meant a great deal to me as I try to apply it to my own life. Every day I complain, I truly spend one more day in the desert, denying myself my Promised Land.

I think the Promised Land isn't just a place. It's also a state of mind. I believe that those who look at life in a very positive, trusting way can enter the Promised Land at any time and stay there. There will, however, always be those who blame the circumstances of their lives on others. For these people, the choice is bondage and slavery.

Victim-itis

"If only-ers" are in danger of becoming professional victims. Some individuals make a career out of blaming others or external situations for their troubles. Since no major villainy has ever been directed at me — I've never been mugged, or been a direct victim of war or extreme poverty — I can't say a whole lot about the experience of being a genuine victim. I do know something, however, about **feeling** victimized, about being persuaded that people, events, or maybe "forces" are out to "get me"!

With me, it is generally "bad forces" which shape events for the express purpose of making me suffer. Let's say I've given a speech and signed all the voucher forms. But the check doesn't come and doesn't come. Anxiety mounts. I finally call the organization in question. It turns out the payment was held up on someone's desk. Or the check was sent to the wrong address. Or maybe the accounts payable clerk is vacationing in Siberia! If this happens to me often enough, I begin to think there's a conspiracy afoot among the gods. Why? Why are they doing this to me?

Actually, nobody is doing anything to me. There are no gods to blame. I am angry at them, at my fate. But it is useless. This is not only useless, it's counterproductive (especially if you gripe within the hearing distance of those involved).

I never get angry at myself. Heaven forbid! That might actually lead somewhere! I might find myself forced to examine my role in the whole mess. I might have to question my choice of vocation, one that is, by its very nature, uncertain. My occasional procrastination of deadlines (okay, let's be honest, it's more than occasional)...my occasional carelessness in thinking I've signed all the vouchers...my failure to fully account for expenses and get them mailed off: all of these might come under closer scrutiny!

Instead, I see myself as a victim. I heave a great sigh of

relief and ponder the injustices of this world. I become self-righteous and mutter something about "unfeeling account-ants" under my breath. (This whole scenario is more than a little embarrassing to admit.)

There are rewards, however! To call ourselves victims is to explain events in a certain way. There are certainly genuine victims. But there are also pseudo-victims who participate in their own victimizations.

It's important to make this distinction. There are those who are perfectly capable of taking care of themselves. But in the presence of others, these people become simpering "jelly fish."

To call yourself a victim is to stake a claim on the sympathy of others. People let others victimize them be-cause to be a victim is to have no responsibility for what happens. It is a claim of innocence, an escape from guilt. "Look what has been done to me."

Self-righteousness follows in the victim's disease pro-cess. To be self-righteous is to feel you can do no wrong. Whatever you do is justified or excused. Even revenge. A person suffers and this gives him permission (or even a per-ceived right) to seek retribution. He believes that an imper-sonal force — Justice, if you will — acts through him. It's his duty to comply. He is merely the agent. The wrath belongs to God.

A victim can achieve genuine moral status, but only by understanding and forgiving the wrong done to him. For-giveness looks within. It sees that we, too, are fully capable of doing harm. If this step is not taken, we can become martyrs, professional victims who always blame others.

There is another option to try when your life is stuck.

This third option always brings you results. I rather suspect it would be the last choice for most of us.

Leave it to Me

OPTION 3 - "If it is to be, then it's up to <u>me</u>."

This choice requires that we seriously look at ourselves. We're the only ones who can change.

With respect to human nature, I'm not convinced that we really "change" anything, least of all ourselves. I think we "exchange" one behavior for another, one feeling for another, or one thought for another.

We can really only be two things and those are what we are now and what we will become. We exchange something today for something in the future. (Our whole economy is built on this process of exchange.) But I will refer to this process as changing ourselves, knowing full well that we are really exchanging a portion of our present self for what we'll be in the future.

<u>Mind Choices</u>

The first thing we can change to alter our lives, is to change our **minds.** We are really mind beings. We do not live in our bodies. We do not live in a city, a state, or in a country that we often identify ourselves as a part of. Rather, we live in our minds.

If we change our minds, we can change our lives. I use the word **attitude,** because we often identify this change of mind with a change in attitude.

There are only two attitudes to choose from. One is negative and the other is positive. Every day we make a decision about where our minds will focus.

There are individuals who get up every day of their lives and plug their one-of-a-kind, unique lives into what I call a "negative socket." These individuals have never seen their lives or the world as anything but a half empty cup.

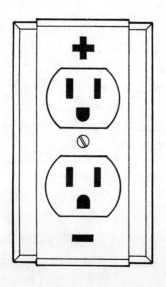

But there are those who get up every day, plug their lives into a positive socket and see their worlds and lives as a cup that is half full. Those who think positively live positive lives. Negative lives surround those who think negatively. Most people are unaware of the awesome power of their minds. We often look at circumstances as the molding forces in our lives. But the truth is that our lives are molded by our minds. **What you think about is what you bring about**. We had better think about how we think. Most of us think by habit.

. . . Ready, Aim, Shoot

If you want to know the sum total of your thoughts, just look at your life today. You certainly were the main architect who made it that way.

Very simply, think of your mind as a camera. It decides what it will focus on. Its ability to focus is an incredible gift. Every morning of your life, you get up and make a decision about where you will put your mind camera for the day. Perhaps you get up some morning and say to yourself, "It's going to be a long day." I can assure you that the moment you made the statement, your body became a supporter of this attitude and you became aware of how tired you were.

Even the body takes orders from the mind. By mid-morning, you probably had enough data in your mind camera to confirm that you were correct in thinking your day would be long and difficult.

Conversely, you might have gotten up and said, "This is a great day." You put film in your camera and found out almost immediately that you had enough evidence to confirm your decision. It doesn't matter if you think you can or can't. You will always be absolutely correct. Your mind will never disappoint you in finding what you set out to find.

I took a trip to the Middle East with a group of friends. I'm not a camera buff, though. And so I made a deal with my friends. I would buy film for them and pay for the development of all their pictures if they would give me one set of prints. In this way I could have a record of everything we had seen and done. They agreed.

A few weeks after my return home, I received a stack of pictures — several inches high. As I sat down to share them with friends, I set aside almost every other photo onto a separate pile. Finally, someone asked me what was pictured in this pile of photos. I told my friends that I hadn't the foggiest idea!

Surprised, they asked, "Well, didn't you go together?"

"Not only did we go together," I answered, "we went to every event together."

We traipsed through every ruin and every cathedral together. Every morning, we got on the bus together and then got off together. We ate together. We even got tired of each other together.

To this day, however, I have photographs of people and places that I've never seen before. Furthermore, I haven't the remotest idea where my friends found the material to take those pictures. I sat back then and realized that our lives work the same way.

We always find what we're looking for. If our minds focus in a certain direction, we will not disappoint ourselves. **Whatever our minds attend to will always be magnified**. It's like putting the zoom lens on a camera.

We probably didn't see any flaws in our mates before we married them. Even if we had, we surely figured we could fix them right up, didn't we? We got them home after the wedding festivities, and put the zoom lens on the camera of our minds.

We began to zero in and focus on those flaws. Lo and behold, before our very eyes, there appeared huge mountains of deficiency. Flaws that we hadn't even seen before. This is true whenever we focus on something. It is clarified and magnified.

Be careful what you think about because you will indeed bring it about. **Where your mind goes, your energy also flows**.

... From a Tiny Seed

We reap what we sow, in kind and quality. We cannot sow thoughts of one kind and expect to reap fruits of another. If you want cabbages in your garden, you don't plant green beans. If you want to enjoy fresh lettuce after harvest, you don't plant carrots, do you? I'm sure you'd also select the best quality seeds on the market, wouldn't you? Your harvest depends not only on the quality of your seeds, but on the careful attention you give to their growth processes. You were never in doubt as to the nature of your product. The cabbages and lettuce will never be green beans and carrots at harvest time. Likewise, you can be absolutely sure that what you express outwardly is the result of your predominant inner thoughts.

We are often told that if we eat right, we will have adequate energy. Eating the right foods certainly does keep the body's mechanism running smoothly. But on any given day when we have upset ourselves or angered ourselves, we find our bodies totally exhausted. It's because our minds also control our energy.

... Remember Chicken Little

Watch your choice of attitude. It could become, as my minister says, your "habitude." You will find yourself in bondage. This is so unnecessary when all you need to do is refocus your camera. Simple, but not always easy.

Whenever you encounter negatively-focused individuals, beware of trying to convince them to change their minds. It seems that after an extended period of negative thinking, a condition called "martyrdom" takes over.

I have a friend whose son maintains that his morning grouchiness cannot change until at least 11 a.m. At this time, he is able to refocus his camera to a better view. For years, the family has accommodated this grouchy morning attitude and literally reinforced it by being gentle and walking on eggs until 11 a.m. every day.

You understand that this young man has made a choice to be grouchy. All of us make this choice from time to time. But to do it repeatedly is to build yourself a habitude. We need to remember **not to play the game with those who have chosen to be convinced about their own lack of choices.**

If you work with one of these individuals — it seems likely that every office or organization has a chronic complainer somewhere — please don't let him or her sit down and get too comfortable when they begin their tales of woe.

Your willingness to listen to the same story over and over only reinforces the behavior. I encourage people to always remain standing when they're accosted by one of these individuals. It seems to shorten the conversations a great deal.

Another successful tactic that you might try is to acknowledge this individual's perception of reality. In other words, don't tell him that his life is really not that bad. When you tell the habitually negative thinker that life isn't as bad as he thinks it is, he will go home and gather proof to substantiate his claim. Libraries of photographs from his mind camera will show you that it truly is as bad as he says. What you should say to such individuals is: "For as miserable as your life apparently is, you are really coping with it amazingly well. I want to know how you have done that."

This remark refocuses the conversation from the negative to the positive. Anyone who has spent that much of his or her life gathering those crummy mind camera pictures has some good things going. For instance, he or she has tenacity, tolerance, perseverance, and patience. I could go on and on.

The characteristics are there. The problem is that negative thinkers focus them in the wrong direction; the traits are plugged into the wrong socket. If they were ever to take these wonderful traits and put them in a positive socket, their lives would be changed.

We all need to be careful when we reflect back over each

day and review the pictures we've taken. As we look at our stacks of pictures, we just might exclaim: "Well, isn't that interesting. My day was just like I thought it was going to be." Chicken Little was right, the sky did fall!

I Just Can't Help It

The second thing you can change about yourself is a **feeling.** As I dealt with clients, I received just as much argument from this suggestion as from any other. Most of us believe our feelings are beyond our control.

Again, we are frequently likely to blame our feelings on others. Someone who makes us mad. Someone who refuses to make us happy. It goes on and on. Our feelings are our choices and they certainly make sense to us to choose them. Sometimes this sense borders on nonsense. Nevertheless, the choice is rewarding to each of us or we would not make it in the first place.

A better assessment of the value of a feeling is not to ask **why** we chose it, but rather **what** does it do for us. All our feelings have rewards. There is some truth to the statement that when we get sick and tired of being sick and tired of being sick and tired, we'll probably exchange one feeling for another.

Let's choose a common feeling and explore for a moment some of its rewards. Most of us are inclined to feel depressed from time to time. I'm certainly not referring to the classification of depression which is chemically induced or which arises as a result of catastrophic loss. But I am referring to a depression based on anger and guilt.

. . . Payoffs

1. For example, perhaps you find yourself getting attention when you're depressed. I used to warn people
   who were positive all the time that they might be
   alone a lot. It seems we don't reinforce or give
   feedback to those who are positive. On those days,
   however, when we're not up to par or are feeling
   depressed, we do indeed attract attention. For some
   of us, this becomes a rewarding cycle.
2. Feeling depressed can buy us time. In fact, listen to
   your language. When was the last time you said, "I'm
   not up to it yet"? In other words, we don't have to
   make a decision because of our depression. We buy
   ourselves some space and time.
3. Depression also entitles us to go on eating binges,
   devouring everything in our refrigerators. Or perhaps depression entitles us to indulge in another
   addiction and the cycle begins. The more I eat, the
   madder I get and the more depressed I become.
4. Perhaps depression also entitles you to control other
   people. I have known individuals who spent a great
   deal of time in a depressed state while their families
   "walked on eggs" so as not to upset them. Sometimes
   it's like sitting in bed and directing traffic as a way of
   controlling others.
5. The choice for depression also entitles us to have "pity
   parties." In fact, I think it's the only party you'll ever

have that nobody really wants to attend. Regardless, we all have them from time to time. I call them my "suck thumb days." We just feel sorry for ourselves and we don't want to deal with life.

Pity parties are a danger since we're the only ones who can begin or end them. I illustrate this concept by visualizing a "pity house." It's the sort of place where we can make choices about what to do with how we feel.

Every time we have a disappointment or a loss of any magnitude in our lives, we must accept that loss and adjust to it. Some people can accept and never adjust. Perhaps there are those who adjust but never truly accept. From the time of your loss or disappointment until you arrive at acceptance and adjustment, there is a "pity house" right smack in the middle of the road.

When those losses come, we have a choice of what to do with that house. We can go around it and get on down the road. Or we can stop in that pity house for a party of sorts.

The pity house has a back door and a front door. When you're in the pity house looking out the back door, you're focusing on your loss. There are individuals who spend years in the pity house, lamenting their losses and becoming bitter in the process.

You do have another choice. That choice is to focus your mind in the other direction. Look out the front door to the future, with hope and expectation. Your life will become more fulfilling.

I once had a client who admitted that she had moved into the pity house. I asked her how long she'd been looking out the back door. She admitted being there for eighteen months. (Each of us is amazingly knowledgeable and aware when we reflect on the rewards we get from our feelings and behaviors.) I asked her how much more time she needed in the pity house. She answered, "About another three months." She knew she wasn't ready to walk outside or to focus her mind in the direction of the future. She was buying herself time and was well aware of it.

When we reflect on our feelings, especially if it's been an upsetting day, we shouldn't ask ourselves, "Why?" Instead, we need to ask, "What did it do for me today to spend my energies in this way?" Our answers tell us how long we will continue with these feelings.

There is a law: "I am that which I feel myself to be." In order to transform ourselves, we must change our inner world through purification of emotions and through right thinking. (More will be said about this process in a later chapter.)

In order to change a feeling, it's necessary to first change the thought that led to that feeling. We tend to develop automatic responses to original thoughts with little or no awareness.

In other words, our reactions to certain thoughts of long-standing duration tend to be habits rather than the result of any conscious assessment. The only alternative to the realization that this is taking place within our thoughts and emotional patterns is to choose a new thought. A thought that provides an antidote to the old one and that leads to more consciously-considered responses.

The third thing we can do when we're stuck is to change a **behavior**. There is a time, I believe, when it's necessary to pick the body up and shove it somewhere. Take action.

Such action is sometimes necessary whether or not our minds are exactly in the right socket or our feelings are as supportive as they could be.

A common misconception is that insight produces change. It does not. It is often instrumental to change, often an essential part of the process. But it does not directly achieve change. Ultimately, it rests with each of us to take action and to say "This _____ is what I want to change."

We are responsible for what we are. We create ourselves by the actions we take. We have done as we have chosen to do. By doing so, we become what we are.

The Charge of the Fight Brigade

It doesn't matter whether you start by changing a thought, changing a behavior, or changing a feeling. You always get a different perspective. When you change your perspective, you have changed.

I have discovered that all of us don't exactly line up to look at ourselves in this introspective manner. In fact, I probably would have fallen off my chair had individuals come in for counseling and said: "You know, my life isn't working well. In fact it's going down the tube. I think it's me." Most of the time individuals complained that their lives were not going well because of something or someone else.

Getting to "10"

I noticed over time that one of the key things in self-assessment and evaluation was that it required emotional pain of some magnitude. We need to feel enough emotional pain before we are willing to risk taking this self-inventory.

If I could do so, I would invent a pain thermometer. I would call it an "Emotional Pain Thermometer." We have one to measure body temperature, so why not a thermometer to measure our emotional resistance? In fact, I've included a drawing of what this pain thermometer might look like.

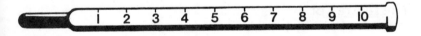

What You Resist Persists

One cannot discuss change without mentioning resistance. Resistance is simply the tendency we humans have to hang on to particular thoughts, feelings or actions before we are willing to risk letting go.

On my pain thermometer, there are ten indicators for pain. Ten is the maximum. At ten, most of us feel we are truly on the brink of disaster. I would challenge you, however, that you are probably on the brink of a miracle. When you transcend ten, you have grown.

It's getting to ten that causes us emotional pain. Whether we are considering an idea, a feeling, or some behavior that we are emotionally attached to, it is often with great resistance that we are willing to exchange it for another. You don't, however, have to be sick to get better!

In other words, you don't **have** to reach ten to risk change. It's just that most of us prefer that the pain and misery come first.

I believe that when you get to ten you will risk change because not risking costs you more. Sometimes life throws us a curve and, lo and behold, we find ourselves at ten without warning. For example: the loss of a loved one, the loss of a job, or some other traumatic event that gives us no warning but requires us to take charge.

<u>Where Are You?</u>

Most of us spend time on the pain thermometer resisting this take-charge opportunity. When people came in for counseling, I always asked them where they were on their pain thermometers. I never worked with an individual who didn't know and couldn't quickly make this assessment.

A man came in one time to figure out how to change his wife. He thought she needed lots of changing but he wasn't having much success on his own. He wondered if I had some ideas. (As I said, the more you nag someone to change, the more you insure he or she will stay the same.)

When we finished our discussion, I told him I really didn't know how to change his wife. But I asked him where he was on his pain thermometer. "When you get to 10," I told him, "you'll change your attitude, your emotions, or your own behavior." He said he was a five.

Now, a five on the pain thermometer means your life is uncomfortable, but it's not yet intolerable. You perhaps do a lot of complaining about it, but very little doing anything about it.

...9-3/4

Another woman came to me who was married to an alcoholic. She told me a tale that would make *As The World Turns* spin. When she finished her story, I told her that when her pain registered at ten, she would take care of herself by either changing an attitude, a feeling, or a behavior.

"Where are you today?" I asked.

She responded, "I'm at 9-3/4."

She was one quarter away from true self-responsibility. But she wasn't ready to risk taking charge. I told her that hers was a terribly painful way to exist. I asked how long she had endured at this level.

With all the pain of a martyr, she answered, "Eleven years."

There's that tenacity I spoke of! It's a need to hang onto a certain aspect of ourselves because we are convinced that we can't ever grow and exchange it for something else.

...1-1/2

A mother called me one day and made an appointment for her son. She wanted me to "fix the kid." Realizing the great challenge of such an assignment, I asked, "Where is your son broken?" When she mentioned that he was 26 years old, I knew I was in big trouble.

She went on to say that he still lived at home. He still had his feet firmly planted under her kitchen table and ate three good meals a day. He slept in a warm bed every night. She said, "Would you believe, I even have to wake him up in the morning to get him to work on time?"

She and her husband were going to send him to me to get him to ten on his pain thermometer. Getting to ten is what good therapy, good parenting, and good self-management is all about. When this young man came in to get fixed and graced me with his presence, it didn't take long to figure out that he probably wasn't going very far. (But he was going there in style and comfort!)

He was a first-class freeloader at this point in his life. He had no drive, ambition, or goals. After about fifteen minutes, when this became clear to me, I said to him: "I want to ask you something. On your pain thermometer today, ten means you're going to move out, get a job, get some direction and take charge of your life. Where are you today?"

He said, "I'm 1-1/2."

I could not have assessed the situation more accurately. When someone is that comfortable, that secure, he will not make any effective changes.

After he left, I called his parents. They, of course, were ecstatic. They thought I had "fixed" their boy in less than fifteen minutes. When they came in, I told them that I really had no suggestions for their son because he was going well...for going nowhere.

"But, Mom and Dad," I said, "when you get to ten on your pain thermometers, you will take the risk. You will put him out on your doorstep. You'll send him on down the road with self-addressed cards and envelopes and a lot of good wishes. Tell him you'll be seeing him and talking to him, but that it's time he take charge of his own life."

Well, mother became livid with me. She informed me in no uncertain terms that she would never do this to her son. If she did, she said, "he wouldn't love me anymore."

It was useless for me to explain that he probably didn't love her that much now. To freeload is not to love.

The point I want to make is that mom and dad — particularly mom — were really the ones in pain. And the one in pain must be willing to take the risk. In changing something about yourself, the risk is in not knowing what the outcome will be. However, when you get to ten, believe me, the risk is worth it.

41

Even though I understand this pain resistance, it has not short-circuited some of the difficult courses in my life. In those instances when I was unwilling to give up my way of doing something or my expectation that something ought to be done a certain way, I had to get to ten. I had to wade through the pain in order to give up, to lose a habit. The paradox is that when I was willing to lose it, I then was able to add on to what I already was. In truth, I didn't give up anything at all. I added more to my storehouse of knowledge.

Problems are nothing more than special delivery messages to us. If there are problems in our lives, it's actually the universe trying to get our attention. The message is that we need to be aware of something or that something needs to be changed.

Life Reflects Our Own Creation

Everybody in our lives is a reflection of our own creation. There are no accidents or events that are unrelated to "me." If I see or feel something that has an impact on me, then my being has attracted or molded it to show me something.

Life is a mirror reflection of our thoughts. We create our lives as we go along. Our experiences and needs give us an instant, ongoing reflection of ourselves.

In fact, the external world is like a giant mirror which reflects our spirits and our forms clearly and accurately. All the people in our lives are reflections of the various characters and feelings that live inside us. That's why everyone who crosses our path is to be considered a teacher.

As I look at my own reflection in the life of another, I can learn, change and grow. Everything is a gift that brings me closer to self-awareness. After all, I'm here to learn. If I was already perfect, I wouldn't be here.

I have also found that when life becomes extremely boring, a person takes charge. This is true of each of us. On those days when we're bored to death, we finally get up and do something about it. I think we take charge sometimes because we see no other choice. When we have a crisis in our lives or a deep spiritual experience that changes our lives dramatically, we are forced to take responsibility.

This book is written on the premise that each of us might choose to change if we knew more and had a bit more understanding about how we're put together, how we mold our lives. This book is also about the tremendous choices we have to make our lives good and full of health, prosperity and abundance.

A Lesson From Nature

It is a full-time job to manage oneself...a lifetime challenge. The conditions and the events of life are not ones that we really have much control over. We can only control 1) our reaction to the things that happen to us and 2) the choices we make. We are never without choice.

Perhaps a story about a colony of little penguins can say it best. When you've finished reading their story, I think you might agree that penguins are really people, too!

Let me set the stage for the story of these little penguins. Evidently, they all began their lives being pretty much equal to each other. They probably enjoyed similar upbringings. They certainly dressed alike (they dressed for success, you know!). And they experienced similar childhoods. All their food had been supplied to them by their parents. They lived in the shadow of a towering wall, quite a distance from the waters. Being so protected and fed, they had plenty of time for play and exploration. They enjoyed life and felt quite secure.

Apparently, their parents went out each day to find food for them. With clock-like regularity, their nourishment was supplied to them. One day, however, their parents realized that to continue to feed them, to protect and shelter them from life was to do them an injustice. Their parents went off, as always, to search for food, but they did not return. It was time to transfer ownership of their lives over to the penguins.

This is what happened to the colony of thirty penguins when life dealt them a "bad hand." They had not anticipated such an event and had not been prepared for it.

As the penguins paced up and down the sand, looking off in the direction taken by their parents, they anxiously awaited the arrival of their food. After all, life had been quite predictable up until this point. It was difficult for them to get on with anything constructive because they stared into the distance, waiting and waiting for life to reappear in its familiar form.

This is true for all of us when life changes. Whether it's a sudden trauma or an anticipated change, there is always a period of grieving for what was. It becomes difficult to internalize what has happened. We cope with it through denial. Some individuals spend a great deal of their lives this way, unwilling to accept what has happened to them.

The Plungers

Anyway, as the penguins continued their pacing, four of them finally decided to take some action. These four separated themselves from the remaining group, never looking back. They waddled off toward the towering wall. After scrambling to the top, where they'd never ventured before, they threw themselves enthusiastically into the water!

We would, I think, see the same results in any group of thirty individuals faced with circumstances beyond their control. There would be four who would grasp the reins of leadership and move forward into the future.

After they leaped into the water, our four leaders found

that, lo and behold, they could swim! We, too, could do great things if we would just "get in the water" and discover our true potential. In these unfamiliar waters, they also discovered all the food they would ever need for the rest of their lives.

These four "penguin people" exhibited many of the characteristics we associate with the leaders among us. When handed an unanticipated set of circumstances, they moved forward because they:

... had a vision. They had the ability to see beyond their circumstances and to see something better on the other side of the wall. It's been written that without a vision, people perish.

... are solution-thinkers. Their minds are focused on the future and on finding a way to solve their dilemma.

... are willing to take risks. They are willing to pursue a solution, to go after what they want.

... are willing to extend their comfort zones and expand their resources.

... have the knowledge that security is internal, not external.

There is nothing external to our lives that we will hang on to or keep. Everything we spend our time and energy on — for example: our families, relationships, career objectives, hobbies, traditions, or money — everything must be given up. The only questions are "How?" and "When?" True security comes from within, knowing who you are and where you are going.

The Leaners

Well, we left those remaining 26 penguins to their pacing on the beach, didn't we? They're getting hungrier and hungrier by the minute. Finally, another six pulled themselves away from the group.

As they cautiously moved away, looking back to what they were leaving behind, they responded to that spirit in their little bodies that propelled them forward. They approached the wall and scrambled a little less assuredly to the top. As they stood there huddled together, they covered their eyes, not wanting to see what they were about to do. Instead of leaping into the water with the enthusiasm of the first four, they merely leaned forward and allowed themselves to fall. After their plunge into the waters, they, too, found food and discovered their ability to swim.

It's interesting to see that within this group of thirty, we have four leaders and six followers. This phenomenon would most likely be mirrored within any group of thirty human beings. There will always be those who follow in the path of others who blazed a trail before them. Followers are not risk-takers. They need to be certain that things have turned out okay for those who led the way. Haven't you found yourself saying, "You go first; I'll be right behind you"?

So, these first ten penguins do deal with solutions and have chosen to get on with their lives. They don't wish to spend much time just waiting for things to get back to the way they were.

The Joiners

The twenty penguins who still aimlessly paced on the sand probably represent two-thirds of our society in the way it reacts to life's unplanned traumas. Finally, nine more left the ranks.

As they moved away, they walked backwards, afraid to lose sight of what they were leaving behind. They became confused, having no sense of the direction they were to take.

Had these been people, I'm sure one would have spoken up and said: "We have a big problem. I think we need to form a committee to discuss our situation." There are a great many individuals within our society who just love to talk about problems. That's why our schedules are so taken up with meetings of one sort or another.

Amazingly enough, this penguin committee did arrive at two unanimous decisions (a very uncommon feat in itself!). The committee first decided it would not go over the wall. After all, they had not seen hide nor hair of the first ten who took that route. Therefore, they must be dead! The second conclusion was that they would only undertake that which they could see was safe. This meant that they would trudge over to a nearby pond. The pond was real and visible to them. It was safe.

These thinkers lack vision. They live their lives through

their senses. If they can't see, touch, hear, feel, or smell something, then it is not real.

As they reached the pond, they tentatively wiggled their little feet into the water. Once assured that it was safe, they eased their bodies into the pond. This group likes to play it safe. You know, if you hang on long enough and don't risk too much, things will eventually return to the way they once were. Comfort zones remain intact and unchallenged for life's "safe players!"

The Wailers

Now we've still got eleven penguins left on the beach. It seemed likely they would starve to death, because by this time they were mighty hungry and disgruntled.

They never really joined forces or banded together. Instead, they wandered aimlessly around in isolation and desolation. They waited for something, anything, to come along and rescue them. In short, these small beings were lost and forlorn.

But, lo and behold, something did come and rescue them! The tide came in and washed the penguins out to sea. They never really had to do anything to find food. They simply went with the "flow" and waited for "the tide to come in!"

You would think this group was ecstatic to find its problem solved with no effort on its part. All the good in life came to the penguins through no fault of their own. But no! Once in the water, the penguins didn't pursue food. They turned their bodies toward shore and scrambled back to land. They stood on the beach, glaring at the water. You almost expected to hear at least one exclaim: "The tide was four days late. Where was it anyway? Heck, it took us where we didn't want to go in the first place." No doubt, a chorus of complaints began and another would surely add: "Well, if we don't want this to happen again without our permission, then we'd better get organized. We need to protect ourselves."

As a result, these little penguins organized themselves in order protect themselves from the tides. They wished to maintain the status quo and protect themselves from the very thing which fed them!

This story, I believe, well illustrates what happens to us with regard to the choices we make in life. Take a moment to consider the options available to the penguin colony. Which group do you think you would have been a part of?

Preparing to Plunge

The following chapters address those areas in which most of our choices are made. If we are to experience life in its full abundance and prosperity, we will make choices in the following areas:

1. How we think.
2. How we view ourselves.
3. How we manage our emotions.
4. How we manage our physical bodies.
5. How we choose our mission.

Most people aren't aware of the awesome management challenge they undertake when they attempt to manage their lives in a positive, constructive way. Are you?

Chapter Two

Control Your Thinking,
Control Your Destiny

If you think you're beaten, you are;
If you think you dare not, you don't;
If you'd like to win, but you think you can't;
It's almost a cinch you won't;
If you think you'll lose, you've lost,
For out in the world you'll find
Success begins with a fellow's will,
It's all in the state of mind. [1]

- Walter Wintle -

The Great Discovery

You are what you think, not what you think you are. You are the manager and the programmer of your mind. Your life depends on how well you do this.

Mankind's first and greatest discovery was that humans could think. From that day on, we became individuals and were forced to take control of our destinies. As a result of this discovery of our capacity to think, plan, and execute plans, we humans perceived that the Life Force had to work through us in order to work for us.

One day, however, some wise man claimed that it was not the brain that did the thinking. His theory was that if the brain did think, it would continue to do so when removed from the body. Yet if the brain is removed, a man does not think. Nor does the brain function independently of its host. This seemed to prove that some force behind the brain plays it like an instrument.

Behind the brain there must be a thinker. Who is that thinker? It is **you**!

By shaping your thoughts, you can mold or re-mold your affairs. By right thinking, you can bring new conditions into your life. Tremendous! Thought is the only mover. According to the degree of your conscious intelligence, you will grasp the power that is yours. Whatever your conscious mind conceives of and you believe in, you will receive.

You can control your thoughts. When you control your thoughts, you control your destiny. You can become as great and as powerful as you conceive of being. You have, at your disposal, the unlimited power of all creation. When you understand this power and use it constructively, you will attract many wonderful experiences into your life.

Most people use only a small portion of their potential mind power. Even worse, many people use the power of their minds to attract negative experiences. The same energy of thought used to attract negative experiences can also attract things that are dynamic and positive. You may ask, "How can I condition my mind to attract good experiences?"

The Master and the Servant

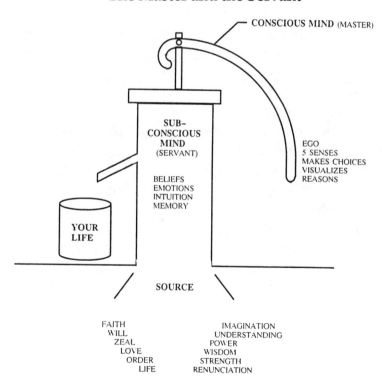

Let's take a look at some of the features of the mind. First, let's talk about its general, overall structure.

Recently, my minister made the analogy that the mind is like a water pump. This pump is constructed on the foundation of a "Source," a Source which is infinite and unlimited in its abundance and potential. Perhaps the comparison is a bit oversimplified, but I like it and have taken some liberties with it.

The Conscious Mind

What is visible and above ground is the body of the pump, its spigot and its handle. The conscious mind, the Master and supreme ruler, is represented by the pump handle. It is the control center, and you are the only one allowed access to it. The conscious mind is self-knowing and self-assertive. It has a will and is able to perceive, to reason, to judge, and to accept or reject. It deals with all the impressions of the visible world that are gathered through the five senses. Because of the decisions our conscious minds make, it is the gateway through which our destinies are realized.

If your conscious mind dwells on negative thoughts such as hate, envy, worry, fear, and anxiety, then what comes through you—or the "spigot" — is despair, poverty, disease, and unhappiness. Conversely, if your thoughts are positive, they, too, will reflect what comes through your spigot. As Paul said, when in the chains of captivity:

"Finally, brethren, whatsoever things are true, whatsoever things are honest, whatsoever things are just, whatsoever things are pure, whatsoever things are lovely, and of good report; if there is any virtue and if there be any praise, <u>think</u> on these things."

The conscious mind is the only part of your mind that thinks independently of conditions around you. It is a finely-tuned instrument whose only task is to assure physical survival. It is as destructible as the body of which it is a part. It has no memory of its own, but simply an ability to recall. It houses some very important characteristics which include the ability to make choices, analyze, and to imagine. It includes the ego, the five senses and above all it is the "master chooser."

<u>Always a Choice</u>

If I say to you, "Don't think of the house where you live," you know that's exactly what you're going to think about. In fact, you'll not think of anything but that house. You immediately think of where the furniture is positioned, how it looks, its size, and on and on. Now if I say to you, "Don't think of all that!" you surely will.

Some time ago, I visited a beautiful area in Colorado's Rocky Mountains. It was a perfect representation of a classic mountain scene, one commonly depicted by artists. All the elements were there: majestic mountains; a serene, calm lake surrounded by pine trees; and fields of breathtakingly beautiful flowers in riotous full bloom.

Now, you've forgotten about where you live, haven't

you? You're thinking now of that beautiful mountain scene, aren't you? I gave you a new and different idea. This is the key to the management of your mind, the management of your thinking and therefore, the key to the management of your destiny.

... Cause and Effect

If you control your thoughts, you control your life. It's simple, but not easy. All of us have developed unique patterns and habits of thought. We observe our outward circumstances and believe them to be the **cause** of our thoughts, rather than the **result** of our thoughts. It is difficult sometimes to comprehend that what happens **to** us began **in** us. The cause is within.

It is vital that we stop to think about **how** we think. Ask a hundred people whether or not their lives have turned out the way they wanted them to. Very few would answer affirmatively. Most people live dissatisfied lives, lives that are unfulfilled in many aspects. But these same people are unable to decide just what those aspects are or how to go about living fulfilled lives. Most people are unaware that their lives are decided by the thoughts they formulate. They believe that circumstances are either beyond their control or that power over these circumstances is gained by an extensive analysis of the situation.

It is a western phenomenon that teaches us to examine external circumstances to find the cause of a problem. This is living backwards. There is no need to apologize for western methods of education. The west has produced its own share of inspirational thinkers and instinctive athletes. I'm only saying that the linear method of thinking, while proven effective in scientific application, is certainly not the only, or even the best, method for individuals to use when they deal with their surroundings. We are bombarded every moment with thousands and thousands of choices which come into the control center of our minds. As the ultimate master, you must choose just one thought at a time.

It has taken mankind thousands of years to learn that we have the power to control our destinies. From the Bible we have the assurance, "As a man thinketh in his heart, so is he." The old Greek philosophers understood something of the meaning of thought: "What we expect," said Aristotle, "that we find." Demosthenes said, "What we wish, that we believe." And Shakespeare, likewise, is credited with saying, "There is nothing either good or bad that thinking makes it so."

It is one thing to **know** a principle, but quite another to **apply** it. What you think about most predominantly will be brought about.

It is difficult to accept that the sum total of our lives today is the result of our thinking patterns. Those patterns led to the current circumstances or conditions of our lives. What we outwardly are and what we are to become depends upon what we think. For everything that happens in the objective world, there must be something in the subjective world that perfectly counterbalances it. We are all immersed in the atmosphere of our own thinking processes. This is the direct result of all we have ever said, thought, or done. This decides what is to take place in our lives. Every thought is a cause; every condition its effect.

Thought attracts what is most like itself. It repels that which is unlike itself. The things accomplished by thought can be undone by further thought. Lifelong habits of wrong thinking can be consciously and deliberately neutralized. An entirely new order of mental and emotional reactions can be established.

It's not enough to merely abstain from **wrong** thinking. There must be active **right** thinking. You must be actively constructive and positive in your thinking, not merely passive and accepting. You must begin right where you are. Never say, "I can't afford this" or "I can't do that." Your subconscious mind takes these statements as direct orders from the "navigator." Instead, say, "I can afford this" or "I can do that." The choices you take are the circumstances you make.

We cannot live a life without choices. In every second of every moment of every day there is a choice to be made. If that weren't the case, we wouldn't be individuals. You have the right to choose what you wish to experience. You have the right to choose the kinds of companions you wish to associate with. You have the right to choose the city or the house you want to live in. Choose only those thoughts you would like to become your reality. The power to choose is one of the capabilities of your conscious mind. As your consciousness expands, your thoughts and choices move on to greater, more dynamic levels.

Analytic Converter

A catalytic converter is that fancy gadget on your auto-mobile whose purpose is to purify exhaust fumes. It converts poisonous fumes into gases that can be safely released into the environment.

Your conscious mind houses a similar contraption that I call an analytic converter. This converter screens the input received from the five senses and interprets it. The events of the outside world are then categorized according to those which produce pleasure and those which produce pain.

The conscious mind remembers which circumstances produced pain and pleasure. It makes this analysis based on past experiences that produced one or the other. It is a recording, an analytical and selective tool of your senses.

Since it is only an instrument of your senses, it is limited by them. It is finite, a thing of this world. It's a structural part of our physical being, without use or purpose once the organism ceases to exist. It records all sensations at the level of pain or pleasure. It analyzes these sensations according to the circumstances that caused them.

It files the sensations away under one of two categories: "Recall About Pain" or "Recall About Pleasure." In itself, the conscious mind has no memory. In other words, it's not the storehouse where all experience and sensation are stockpiled. The subconscious mind is the warehouse of memory. The conscious mind can only recall certain experiences and conclusions that have previously been recorded.

The true power of the conscious mind lies in the conclusions it makes based upon analysis. Imprinted on the subconscious mind, these conclusions are reflected in our lives.

Dream Big

The most powerful gift of the conscious mind is that which follows our choice of thought. For every thought you think, pictures are made. Your life will never exceed your thoughts or the pictures generated by these thoughts. You have an imagination and it's a good one. You use it every day of your life, but you may not use it as effectively as you might.

With your imagination you can mold and shape your life. You can dream of the things you would like to experience. You can dream about the places you would like to go, the education you would like to have, the harmonious relationships you would like to enjoy.

You don't have to wait until the external circumstances of your life indicate that some of these things are possible. It is the constructive and creative use of your imagination, in visualizing these things, that makes them possible. One reason many people lead unproductive lives is that their lives are largely the product of an unconscious, negative use of the imagination. These unfulfilled people used their wonderful gift of imagination to picture themselves as limited in health, wealth, and achievement. As the mind sees, the body experiences. Vision, conscious or unconscious, always precedes experience.

It's astonishing when we realize how we let others influence our imagination and its use. Instead of visualizing our dreams, we visualize the negative opinions of others and their projections. We visualize what we see in and about us, rather than what we'd like to see and experience. Instead of looking at our lives from a human point of view (and then reinforcing this view with imagination), we should see our lives as we'd like them to be.

See yourself doing the work you'd most like to do. When you receive ideas that feel right for you, visualize those ideas in your mind. Don't put them aside, thinking they are too big to accomplish. It takes big dreams to accomplish big things. Be bold and fearless.

Any idea given to you by the Source must be possible to achieve. Imagination is the architect of the mind. Whatever thought structures we build and believe in, we can make real in our lives. The purpose of this architect we call "imagination" is to construct mental images and to impress these images on the subconscious mind. Only in this way can the subconscious mind work with some creative plan or direction.

In his book **Psycho-Cybernetics**[2], Dr. Maxwell Maltz tells of his discovery of how powerful our imagination is in the direction and leadership of our minds. As a plastic surgeon, Dr. Maltz rebuilt the features of many people, making them look beautiful on the outside. He discovered that the lives of many were transformed by their renewed outer appearance. But many others — no matter what changes were made on the outside — still viewed themselves as unattractive. These people saw an "inside" picture, the one in their imaginations. Dr. Maltz determined that we too often operate from the mental images we create in our imaginations.

The anorexic supplies us with another classic example of the distortion of a person's inner picture when compared to external realities. The anorexic may be skin and bones, but will still see an obese individual in the mirror. Your life will never exceed the scope of the pictures you make in your mind.

... It's Your Movie - The Sequel

If you asked a group of individuals, "Have you ever thought about what success looks like?" each person would have a totally different description. One of the most frustrating things in my own life, as well as in the lives of those I have worked with, is the discovery of how limited our pictures are.

Even though an idea might be tremendous and dynamic — in the sense of our choice of thought — the mind frequently diminishes it to a picture of microscopic proportions. As a result, our lives are filled by limitations and lack.

One of the most phenomenal discoveries of mankind is that the subconscious mind, the servant, reproduces the pictures taken by the master, the conscious mind, without question. Those mental movies that we design, write the script for, and direct, are the products of our own creative imagination.

Take a good look at your life. It's exactly as you pictured

it would be. It is the sum total of all the pictures you have ever taken.

Your future, however, lies within your control, even yet. Believe in your dreams. See yourself creatively expressing your talents and good desires. Keep your dreams to yourself. Do not subject them to the negative analysis and discouraging scrutiny of others. Cherish your dreams and nourish them with a strong belief. If you give them room to live within you, you will see them reflected in your life.

It takes courage to imagine yourself as successful at something that seems beyond your presently perceived ability. It also takes courage to see yourself as prosperous, to think of yourself as affluent when you may be down to your last dollar and in debt. The old visions of limitations challenge these new, bold dreams.

DO NOT be deterred in your efforts. **DO NOT** resist the old vision. Just calmly deny it. Affirm only positive thoughts and suggestions. Do this repeatedly. Do it especially when circumstances suggest to you something negative or limiting. It is most difficult visualizing and imagining success when outer appearances seem contradictory.

Your thoughts and pictures of today are the realities of your tomorrow. Your movie is written, cast, directed, and produced by you. How do you envision your future? What kinds of pictures do you have of success?

. . . The Magic Within

Remember the story of Aladdin and his magic lamp? Aladdin found an old lamp unnoticed by others for centuries. He discovered that when the lamp was rubbed, a genie appeared. This genie granted the owner any and all wishes.

When you were little, you probably fantasized about how wonderful it would be to have such a magical lamp. You're about to find out there is just such a magical power at your disposal right now. Your own all-powerful genie is actually your subconscious mind. It has the power to bring about your every desire, no matter how great.

If this is true, then why are so few people content with their lives? The simple fact is that most people don't begin to live up to their full potential.

The potential of every human being can be compared to a building designed to soar one hundred stories. Most of us only build two stories. The occasional venturesome soul dares to add a third. We confine ourselves to a limited existence when we could build on and on and up and up. We are the engineers who can make this possible.

When compared to the subconscious mind, the conscious mind only has the meager power, heat, and light of a candle. You might wonder why we should concern ourselves at all with such a small portion of our minds.

The conscious mind remembers only a few years and a very few facts. It has barely mastered the rudiments of thought and is scarcely capable of dealing with its immediate surroundings. In order to process all that our conscious minds are capable of, we have only five tools at our disposal: sight, hearing, taste, touch, and smell.

The power of the conscious mind lies in the master and servant relationship it enjoys. As startling as it may seem, this tiny, little conscious mind is the master of your life.

The Subconscious Mind

The servant, your subconscious mind, is illustrated as the body of a pump. It's that portion which connects the Source to the handle. The subconscious mind represents the laws of the Universe in action. It is not a thing in itself.

It does not think, reason, balance, judge, or reject. It simply accepts all the input furnished by the conscious mind. It matters not at all whether the suggestions are good or evil, constructive or destructive. It merely is the medium for all thought and action. Herein lies the mighty power of the conscious mind.

The subconscious mind is the infinite substance of which all things are made. It has no beginning and no end. Everything exists within it. It knows everything and is everything. Time and space are irrelevant. It is everywhere at all times and all of it is anywhere at any given time.

The subconscious mind has the power to heal the body, to create physical form and physical circumstances. It is an abstract and formless state. It is potential energy and latent power. This means it is unformed, but always ready to take form. It is ready to be formed into any and all forms.

It is unexpressed power. It waits to be called into form or expression. It is always willing, but has no volition of its own. Because it possesses no initiative, it waits for direction from the conscious mind.

We all are familiar with the massive power of the elephant. An elephant can pick up a one-ton load with its trunk. Have you ever visited a circus and seen these enormous creatures standing quietly while tied to small wooden stakes? Did you never wonder how this seemingly miraculous feat was accomplished?

When young and relatively weak, the baby elephant is secured by a heavy chain to an immovable iron stake. Later in life, no matter how large and strong the elephant becomes, it continues to believe it cannot move while fastened to any stake in the ground — regardless of what material secures it.

Many intelligent people are just like these circus elephants. They are limited in thought, action, and results. They never question the limitations imposed upon them. They never wonder "Who?" "Why?" or anything else. Are you still tied to your limited thinking patterns? Your subconscious will fulfill the exact expectations of your program until you, its Master, rewrite the program.

The Original Computer

The subconscious mind functions somewhat like a computer. It waits for the conscious programmer to make choices which the computer implements without question. It is useless without these instructions. The subconscious has tremendous capabilities to process information, to problem-solve, and to recall data at will.

The subconscious mind functions very much like the computer in your own office or work place. The programs fed into your subconscious actually direct everything in your life: your emotions, habits, relationships, health, and your financial situation.

Over ninety percent of your mental life is subconscious. It's on the job twenty-four hours a day. The only part that sleeps is your conscious mind. From the time you were born to the present, your subconscious has accepted and stored a wealth of information. It serves as a warehouse for everything that has ever happened in your life: everything you've ever felt, all your successes and failures, all your happiness and unhappiness. We've all grown up with ideas about ourselves that are negative, inaccurate, damaging, and outdated.

Over the years, these self-defeating ideas persist. They are easily available for immediate recall. You might remember a statement I made earlier: "You are what you think, not what you think you are." This doesn't simply refer to what you **know** you think. It also refers to what you **don't know** you think.

For example, you may be unaware that deep in your subconscious lies the belief that you are unworthy, that you don't deserve lasting, loving relationships or financial success. Is it any wonder that you don't have satisfying relationships or a healthy bank balance? Your subconscious mind exerts its influence over your life more than you realize.

Many people wonder why the subconscious mind accepts negative input in the first place. After all, don't we want the best for ourselves? But the subconscious mind accepts ideas and beliefs without question, and impacts our lives accordingly.

Our habits and belief systems extend into every part of our lives. What do you believe about your health? Do you experience at least one good cold each winter only because you expect it? The real cause is your belief that you will become ill; the cold symptoms are merely symptoms of your expectations.

I often ask my seminar participants to verbalize some of their beliefs about health. I hear such responses as, "I've never been in very good health" or "My family all die young." A few rare individuals might claim, "I'm never sick," and it's true that they rarely are!

Even our home remedies or cures are often deeply embedded in our subconscious minds. They work because we believe they will. Placebos of our own making! Two office colleagues recently shared with me remedies from their growing-up years. For a sore throat, one gargles with salt water; the other drinks tea with lemon juice and honey. And in spite of the vast array of antibiotics on the market today, both colleagues agreed that if they really wanted to be sure, they did what "really cures."

We also have belief systems relative to our financial situations. If you believe you don't deserve wealth and that you are destined to live on the edge, your genie sets out to confirm these beliefs. It never questions. "We always have to work for our money," "We'll never be rich," "We'll always just get by," "The rich have all the problems," "We never have more than enough," "Save it for a rainy day": these negative thought patterns are never converted by your subconscious mind to anything more positive. It takes your orders seriously.

This principle works in every aspect of our lives. My friends are greatly amused as I use the law to find parking places. Whenever I'm out driving, I always believe there is a parking spot just waiting for me. And of course, this spot is directly at the entrance of my destination. Those people who ride with me and humor me do so because they <u>don't</u>

believe it possible (and also because they don't want to walk very far, either!). What do you know? It works! What do you say or think to yourself when you approach a parking lot? I'll bet it's, "I'll never find a place to park."

... Limit/Expand

Some of our belief systems are extremely self-limiting and cause us great emotional turmoil. There are others, however, that are very positive because they move us to higher and greater things. The system works to either limit or to expand our lives. It is impersonal. Our beliefs create the facts around us.

In our quest for wealth and success, we concentrate mainly on external, tangible considerations. We look for breaks, business opportunities, marketing strategies, creative ideas, wise applications of business know-how, profitable investments, and just about everything else under the sun.

William James, dubbed the father of American psychology, advised that belief creates the actual fact. All this means is that your innermost attitudes, beliefs and thoughts are responsible — more than any other factors — for success or failure. Your beliefs become the energy that makes persistence, patience, and determination pay off. They are the keys to the kind of life you've only dreamed of.

While some seem to know automatically that they will succeed, others expect the worst in spite of their conscious desire for success. These negative expectations place limits and restrictions on our accomplishments. They keep us constantly struggling, frustrated, and unhappy. They arise from the subconscious mind, perhaps the single most important determiner of our lives. Such conditions are orders faithfully carried out by our servant, the subconscious mind.

You can keep your potential locked away behind walls of limited thoughts, or you can take charge now and restructure your subconscious. You can build higher on the building that is your life. Then you will reap your rewards! Fortunately, negative subconscious beliefs can be changed.

Knowledge From Within

Knowledge within the subconscious is called intuition. It's light-years ahead of what your conscious mind can grasp. Intuition is the power of knowing. It is most often accompanied by a recognition that our insight is a fact, that our intuition is true. Although we do not know how we know it — and we may even doubt our own feelings of its truth — these insights and feelings often turn out to be accurate.

Such feelings, or hunches, include thinking of someone who then calls or visits, having a major insight on how to solve a particular problem, or finding exactly the right strategy to implement a communications project. Most of us have had such an experience.

The first step to enhance our intuitive abilities is to be vigilant in recognizing flashes of intuition or insight. One way to become more adept at recognition is to sit back, relax, and close your eyes. Then, ask yourself to think back and re-experience your latest insight. It might have been a flash prompting you to recheck the oven settings or a feeling that you would hear from a certain individual in the near future. Perhaps your flash occurred in a dream, during meditation, or maybe while you relaxed in a hot bath. (Bathrooms, for some reason, are great breeding grounds for intuition!) For me, intuitive insights come most often while I'm shopping in a grocery store or driving.

... A Question of Truth

An immediate concern of people who start developing and becoming more aware of their intuition is the question of "truth." The question is best answered by the voice of one's personal experience. A high degree of integrity is required to determine which is conscious, wishful thinking and which arises from our innermost Source of knowing.

Ask yourself how much you trust this insight. How much confidence do you have in it? Put the insight aside for a few days and come back to it. Does it still seem as exciting as it first did?

Take a look at your motivations. There is a different quality and texture to hopeful self-delusion and the peaceful, knowing certainty of intuition. When it's right, you know it!

Intuition allows us to see without eyes and to hear without ears. It is not instinct. Instinct is merely the self-preservation principle inherent to all life forms. Intuition leads to a conviction and to the realization of your true being and your true Source.

... Responding to the Itch

I have made many large and small decisions in my life. Ultimately, the timing and knowledge necessary for these decisions came to me through intuition. I am a risk-taker. I believe that to live life to its fullest, we must take risks. Without risks, our lives become stale and limited in comparison to our potential for fulfillment and success.

I have started my life over, practically from scratch, four times. Each time, I just **knew** it was meant to be. I first recognized, what I call, an "inner restlessness." I have since learned to refer to this restlessness as "God scratching." There comes a time to grow, and this scratching is the first indicator that changes are in the works.

After heeding this indicator and using my conscious mind to analyze data available to me through my five senses, I would just wait. I waited until I had a sense of **knowing** the specifics of the timing or the direction of the changes to be made.

The last move I made was so clearly right for me. I knew I could trust my inner knowledge and depend on the fact that it would always be for my highest good. I had known for about a year that it was time to close my private practice and move to a city where I had access to a larger airport. (I was doing a great deal of public speaking which demanded that I travel quite a distance. It seemed only right that such a move be made.)

At the completion of a program I was presenting in April of that year — in the very city I had determined would be my new home — a fellow in the audience asked, "When are you going to move here?" With no conscious thought,

"November 1" popped out of my mouth.

I backed away from the podium in surprise at my declaration. I was somewhat startled by this date. It had just seemed to come to me from within. I knew it was right.

I returned home, closed the private practice and sold my house. On November 1 of that same year, I pulled into the city I had chosen as my home base. I may have had that sense of knowing, but I had little else!

I had no place to live, no office, and no clientele to justify the move. Still, I knew that the timing and the move itself were right for me. In time, all the unknowns fell into place.

I have learned to trust this sense of knowing. It's not the timing we usually tend to make our decisions by. It's not the clock or the calendar. Instead, it's knowledge and timing that comes from a Source which truly knows what is best. I use this intuition in even the smallest aspects of my life.

Sometimes, intuition appears as a thought that pops into your head. For example, you might have the thought to get an extra car key made. Or perhaps you think to double check something you had previously thought was complete. Within days you find your car keys locked in the car or discover that you didn't sign an expense voucher. I'm learning to respond and take action when these thoughts arise. In retrospect, when I did not act, I suffered the consequences.

The Center of Emotion

Your subconscious mind doesn't react to words alone. The words — our wishes, goals, and beliefs — must be emotionalized, they must be charged with enthusiasm.

75

Our wishes must be programmed with a burning desire, with wild imagination, mental picturing and expectation. The computer in your subconscious is highly sensitive to your emotions, wishes and expectations.

There are two emotional states: positive and negative. Deeply lodged in the subconscious are mental blocks, complexes, grudges, the unwillingness to forgive, hate, habits, self-image concepts, positive and negative patterns, character traits, and feelings of love. In other words, your total life experience.

When positive, unexpected, pleasant and happy feelings suddenly overwhelm us, we probably take them for granted and simply revel in the positive feedback. On the other hand, when negative unexpected, unpleasant and unhappy feelings suddenly overwhelm us, we struggle with our fears, angers, and tensions. We probably interpret the negative forces to have come from outside ourselves. We're certain they're not of our own doing. We're not aware that they are the direct result of a negatively programmed subconscious.

Habits — whether they be thought or behavior patterns — are so hard to break because of the emotional baggage accompanying each pattern. We can consciously, rationally, and logically know what is best for us and still find ourselves "stuck" emotionally.

... What is it That Never Forgets?

What else, besides the great elephant, never forgets? The subconscious mind is a vast storehouse of knowledge, particularly memory. By the time you are thirty years old, you have stored approximately three million mental movies in your subconscious mind. Some of those memories are outside conscious recall. But the emotional overtones of an unremembered incident or experience often continue to impact our lives. Nothing goes unrecorded by the subconscious mind. It also houses all the police systems that govern life, including habits.

... With Flying Colors

Let's look at a case involving Steve. Steve had a programmed belief in his subconscious "computer" that said he was not a good student and certainly not smart enough for college. At one point in his high school days, a math teacher told him that he was not "college material."

This early programmer suggested that he plan to "work with his hands." Therefore, the teacher advised him to transfer from an advanced math class to a more general course. The teacher also suggested to Steve that he take industrial arts courses in preparation for a career which didn't require college work.

Once this statement was made, it went directly into the computer of Steve's subconscious mind. He never questioned its logic. (Remember, once the computer is programmed, it asks no questions and needs no additional confirmation or verification of its data.)

He did exactly what his teacher suggested. He graduated from high school wondering what he would do to prepare himself to make a living. He, too, believed he was not college material. Fortunately, he had an inner spirit that came through — as it does for many of us — in the form of desires, dreams, and ambitions.

His desire was to be a carpenter or builder. It was far more powerful because it came from the Source of his being. It moved him forward to enroll in a building trades program at a junior college. Even this was cause for apprehension, because his computer program said he was not even junior college material!

He stuck with it and finished the program with flying colors. Because of his successful performance, there was now a discrepancy between his inner programming and his external performance. When this happens, we have to correct the discrepancy.

He corrected himself by saying that his excellent performance was "just luck." He never allowed himself to glory in his abilities. He felt that anyone could pass this program because, after all, he was able to! Before long, he rationalized away his earned performance by talking himself out of his success. By this means, his emotional programming could remain intact and unchallenged.

Steve went on to build houses. But the dream persisted for something more. To be the builder he wanted to be required a college degree in engineering. The computer program was immediately activated and said, "But you're not college material." The desire and the spirit prevailed once again. He enrolled in the college of engineering at a major state university and, after much emotional trauma and anxiety, he received his degree.

The tug-of-war that Steve experienced was not with his intellectual potential. It was with his emotional programming. Some of the most difficult times were when he'd wake up in the silence of the night and consciously think of all that had to be done. At these times, the old emotional program was prone to rear its ugly head!

He could even recall — clearly and precisely — the very words his high school math teacher used to tell him he was not college material. After so many years, these words continued to follow his every footstep and to invade his every thought. He had to consciously talk himself into walking into those classes on many days because, emotionally, his program felt that he shouldn't be there.

Even achieving his degree didn't seem to completely quiet that subconscious voice. It seemed he still doubted his true abilities.

After one more degree, he truly was able to challenge that original negative program. (Even that degree, though, he felt was something of a fluke.) After more than ten years of buying into the original program, he was able to write a new one that indicated he was justified in the pursuit of his degrees.

That genie and the emotional programming give up very reluctantly because they are adamantly convinced of their absolute rightness. They persist in their pursuit of your dreams until they prove they are right.

You know, that math teacher was probably a very fine individual, just like you or me. He suffered, though, from a sadly lacking understanding of his power to program. We all need to be aware of the power we have to impact the lives of others and act accordingly. Never has "do unto others as you would have them do unto you" had so much meaning!

The Source

Below the level of the subconscious mind is the True Source. The mind of man is part of this Source. Since the dawn of human existence, and through all succeeding ages, mankind has recognized a mighty, invisible force that governs and controls the universe — a power by which and through which all things are created. Some have personalized this power and named it God.

The Source contains unlimited possibilities for expansion and self-expression. The Source is infinite and the mind of Man is part of this infinity.

The human mind continuously unfolds into a greater recognition of its real plan in the creative order of the Universe. It does not yet comprehend its power or scope. But it does know how to consciously cooperate and align itself with this infinite Source where all true knowledge resides.

The Powers That Be

In his book, **Twelve Powers of Man**[3], Charles Fillmore suggests that your conscious mind possesses twelve wonderful gifts from the Source. These are mental faculties available to you with no limitation. When you balance these gifts in your everyday life, you will find inner peace and perfect harmony — both within yourself and throughout your world.

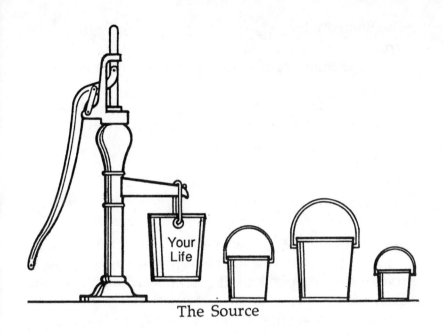

The Source

Faith
(perceive the invisible)

Imagination
(vision beyond appearances)

Will
(permission giver)

Understanding
(knowing with your heart)

Zeal
(enthusiasm)

Power
(heart and mind are one)

Love
(knowing oneness with all)

Wisdom
(intuition)

Order	Strength
(proper sequence of mind,	(patience)
body and affairs)	
Life	Renunciation
(progress, mastery	(releasing negativity)
and attainment)	

Stand Up and be Counted

At workshops and elsewhere, I have often asked the question, "Who are you?" The response is usually one of puzzlement. People think it is an absurd and irrelevant question.

A woman responds, "I am a wife and mother."

"No," I reply, "You have only described your roles. That is not who you are." (Remember, there are thirty-five to fifty roles that we play!)

A man says, "I have spent thirty-eight years as an insurance agent. I live and breathe the business. As far as I'm concerned, this and being a good father, church member, and decent citizen is identity enough."

He has named his vocation, not his identity.

Someone else responds, "I am mind and body."

"You left out soul," adds another.

"All right, so I'm mind, body, and immortal spirit. And I have a role as worker, parent, and citizen. How's that?"

It's easier to define what you are **not**:

You are not merely a physical body, for that is temporal

and will one day cease to exist.

You are not parent, child, employee, or employer. These are roles and relationships.

Who am I? I am a center of pure consciousness. I am a part of the Divine Essence. I am, at the core of my being, made of the same spirit and essence which the Source is composed of. As a child consists physically of the same blood and tissue as his parents, so am I a child of the Source.

I am a being who is "aware of being." A self who is aware of being a self as no other animal can be. I am an individual expression of that true Source. I am an infinite spirit encased in a finite body that will eventually return to dust. Whether we call this inner awareness self, spirit, soul, or a portion of the Divine Essence, we are simply groping for finite words to express the infinite.

A Rose by Any Other Name...

It doesn't matter what we call anything. The only thing that matters is whether or not we have the right idea about the thing which we want to name.

If the meaning of life is to grow and fulfill our destinies, then the ultimate meaning of life is to accept and bring into harmony both our humanity and our divinity.

I have difficulty in fully accepting my humanity. And I cannot completely accept my divinity. There are many aspects of my humanity that I reject or dislike. Thus, I am not fully human. All self-rejection is based in part on

83

rejection of one's humanity.

It is even more difficult to accept, on a feeling level, the astounding premise of our divinity.

Referring to the illustration of the pump, I am in part an individualization of the Source. Yet I am not the Source. It is this connection that entitles us to claim our "pound of worth" (as will be further discussed in Chapter Three). It is not ours as a result of any human accomplishment.

Take Control

We were given freedom and ownership over the inner realm of our being. We have been instructed with a portion of Divinity. We are in charge!

But there are limitations imposed on us by our genetic wiring and environmental conditioning. For instance, I could never have become a mathematician, a nuclear physicist, an opera singer, or a concert pianist. Nor can I fly by flapping my arms, a limitation imposed on me by physical laws.

However, within the framework of my self-hood, I am in charge. I am responsible for what becomes of me, for what I do to others, and for my ultimate destiny.

The struggle is first to accept our humanity and our divinity. Then we must merge them. Thus, these two warring selves will eventually be united in harmony. Most people want no interference from the Source except when a crisis arises. In other words, they prefer to go it alone, relying only on their humanity.

When I'm on a plane approaching an airport, I always

hope the pilot is willing and anxious to listen to instructions from the traffic controller! When contacting the tower for instructions, the pilot does not limit his self-hood. The survival of all on board the plane depends on his complete and perfect obedience to instructions.

Thus at any busy airport, planes regularly land and take off following predetermined flight plans which include altitude and timing factors. The directions and commands issued from the tower do not limit the freedom of the pilot in any way. He is free to ignore them at the risk of grave consequences.

For Goodness' Sake

All the resources available within the Source are not, in any way, meant to infringe on our freedom or autonomy. Rather, they make certain that our lives are more abundant and more harmonious. Only good comes from the well. We are masters of our fates and rulers of our inner kingdoms. Our welfare and happiness depends on how well we obey and understand the principles given to us for tapping the well. All the good that's meant for us must come through us.

There is something in us that urges us onward and upward. It is that part of us which aspires to do more, to be more, to achieve more, to love more, and to grow emotionally and spiritually. I believe this upward stretch of the soul is not encapsulated in that portion of us designated as spirit. Instead, this growth principle resides in every cell, atom, and molecule of every living thing. Growth is the meaning of life. Whatever enables growth is good. Anything limiting growth is evil. (Evil is "live" spelled backwards.)

We are not accountable for what was done to us by parents or other environmental factors. But we are responsible for becoming the highest and best under our unique circumstances. Whatever our limitations or endowments, we are in charge of our own lives and destinies. We need to keep growing.

The Spigot and the Bucket

What comes to you must come through you. The good that is yours from the Source must pass through your subconscious mind in the form of beliefs (originally programmed by the conscious mind). Our good can be blocked. Rust and corrosion in the body of the pump can hinder its smooth passage. (Chapter Four deals more fully with what clogs and keeps the good from us.)

Our challenge is to keep the passage open and clean so that all that is waiting for us and in us is moved along. We need to align ourselves with the Source through positive thinking. Then we can become a channel through which pours all the forms and dimensions of our self-expression.

Imagine a bucket at the spigot of your pump. It is of whatever size or shape you choose. It is your life. The only factors that limit the capacity of your bucket are your thoughts. Imagine having all the Universe at your disposal and, by your own habit of thought, you choose to exist in a soap bubble. To never tap the well is to be like the heir of a great fortune who chooses to live in abject poverty.

In Review

The **CONSCIOUS MIND**, or the "pump handle":

- The master programmer of your life, body, environment, and affairs.

- The gateway through which your destiny arrives.

- The maker of choices which accepts or rejects, analyzes, judges, reasons, and is assertive. It must decide whether or not to pump.

- The image maker and architect of your future.

- Thinks independently of external conditions.

The **SUBCONSCIOUS MIND**, or the connecting pipe between the handle and the Source:

- The servant.

- Does not think, reason, balance, judge or reject. It simply accepts any blueprint and never argues.

- Never forgets.

- Solves problems.

- Houses all habits and beliefs.

- Impersonal computer. Carries out all programming provided by the master programmer.

- Limits or expands.

- Gives unlimited knowledge or intuition.

- The center of emotion.

The **SOURCE**, or the well beneath the pump:

- Contains mental faculties which are unlimited.

- That which pushes us onward and upward.

- The divinity within.

- The mighty invisible force behind and within all of us.

The **SPIGOT**:

- An extension of the subconscious mind through which all is manifested.

- The externalization of your thought processes.

The **BUCKET**:

- The evidence of your life.

- You determine the size and shape...it's your choice!

...It Does Not Compute...

Let's talk now about how to reprogram the computer. We want to reprogram our computers to have greater access to the awesome power of the Source, a power which is equal to the heat, light, and might of the sun.

Proper Protocol

• The first step is to **RELAX**.

It's the first and most crucial step in making any self-help program work for you. Through relaxation, the subconscious mind is directly accessed.

Normally, the conscious mind acts as a pseudo-filter for the subconscious mind. Information must pass through it before entering the subconscious. To get directly to the subconscious mind, you must take measures to bypass the conscious mind. Relaxation accomplishes this very thing. It acts as a kind of psychological doorway, opening the way for you to change your thought patterns and your life.

Relaxation, in this case, does not mean reading a book or watching TV. Rather, it refers to the systematic release of anxieties and muscular tensions. Stress and tension dissolve while the mind focuses. Sound familiar? It's been referred to as meditation but is actually any systematic method leading to reduced tension and anxiety in the body and mind. Such methods allow the conscious mind to be relieved of distractions. Then the mind can focus on positive programming.

One of the best relaxed mental states is the period just before falling asleep — the drifting stage. It occurs again just after you wake but are not yet completely alert. You also experience this state when driving your car on a monotonous stretch of road, staring out the window in a trance-like state. Many people already experience this state of consciousness. Yet they do not realize their minds are receptive to reprogramming at these times.

• The second step is **DESIRE**.

Our subconscious mind is a powerful magnet which can attract from the Source all we want or need. Don't be afraid to ask for a car, a new house, positive relationships with others, etc. These requests must be things you actively **desire**, not merely things you **wish** you had. There is no limit to what the Source can give you. The only limitation is within you. The only restriction arises from your inability to believe all the good that is available to you. Your bucket is too small!

90

• The third step is to **AFFIRM** and **VISUALIZE**.

You must affirm and visualize your desire with intense feeling, with strong mental pictures of the desire. You must mentally **see** and **feel** the accomplishment of your goals. Some people have difficulty with visualizing mental images. These images may be difficult for them to construct. Other images, based on other senses, may be comparatively easy for them to construct. For instance, some people may find it easier and better to imagine auditory or tactile impressions and to concentrate on these. Also, taste and smell — or any combination of sensory impressions — help to create an image which may not be visual in nature at all.

When we reproduce mental impressions, the intensity of sensation varies greatly between individuals. Some people can actually cause sensations of color or sound within themselves. Usually, there are certain better-loved colors or sounds that the subconscious mind recalls from previous experience and reproduces more effectively than others.

A. Make your affirmation short and positive.

What do you want to change? If you wish to have more confidence, affirm, "I am confident." If it's strength, "I am strong." Should you wish to improve your health, "I am well and full of energy," would suffice. Consider how often you affirm, "I am sick," "I am weak," or "I am afraid." Whatever follows, "I am..." is exactly what you are. You can have it either way.

Your subconscious computer does not convert negative into positive. It is a literal system with no sense of humor. Avoid such words as lose, not, don't, won't, never, and so on. "I will not be sick" is likely to be heard by the computer as "...be sick."

B. State your affirmations in the present tense.

The subconscious computer knows no past or future. It only understands the present. It's, "I am well and full of energy today," not, "Someday I'll be well and full of energy." Using the future tense assures that your message will be erased before it even enters the computer. The moment you make your affirmations, they exist in your psychic reality.

C. Repeat, repeat, repeat.

As you get into the habit of repeating positive affirmations, they will probably sound a little strange at first. But you must repeat an affirmation until you believe it and your computer's reprogramming is complete. Beware of the internal voice that challenges your positive statements. Once more, it's only the critic rearing its ugly head! If doubts creep in, just gently push them aside. Don't give them a foothold by dwelling on them. Any thought, positive or negative, dies from a lack of attention.

D. Write them down.

Place your statements of affirmation on a mirror or some other place that you see on a regular basis. If you can utilize all five senses in your reminders, both concretely and in your imagery, that ability will greatly accelerate your reprogramming process. Everything begins with a desire. Fuel it with passion. See it in vivid technicolor. Hear it as loudly as you can tolerate.

• The fourth step is **BELIEF**.

You must believe completely in your power to reprogram your subconscious mind. Expect that your new program is at work immediately. We are told by many psychologists that for every doubt you have, seven positive statements are required to neutralize it.

This belief is comparable to the task of planting a seed in a garden. If you go out every day and pull out the seed to see if it has grown, you will kill whatever new growth has taken place. It cannot flourish until it is allowed to complete the natural process.

This is also true of an idea or a desire. Be assured that when you are ready, your harvest will come. Your desire will have become a reality in your life. Trust and know that it is done according to your belief.

Repetition is the key. The subconscious computer wants to be sure that you really expect this thing and really mean it. Repetition is imperative. See the finished product amplified by all your senses.

Let your subconscious bring about your desire in its own way. As soon as your desires are programmed, you must cultivate a positive state of mind. You must believe that your desires are already accomplished.

Do not worry about its coming. Your positive mental attitude will be suppressed, blocked, congested, delayed, or distorted when negative thoughts creep in. Stress, fear, doubt, anxiety, and frustration block your goal. "I wonder when it will come." "I wonder where it will come from." "I wonder how it will come." These questions nullify all the good previously done with positive programming. Avoid such questioning thoughts as you would the plague!

• The fifth step is to **TAKE ACTION**.

Do everything you can to get ready for your affirmation to materialize. Whatever you desire, visualize it in technicolor and expect it. It surely won't arrive one day without you doing everything you can to manifest it. That means you work for it and save money for it. To bring it about, you prepare for it with your own efforts. Get ready!

Do all you can to get ready. Then just wait until the door clearly opens and your desire comes to you without any additional effort on your part.

• The sixth step is **CONVICTION**.

Know that you know. Release it. Forget about it. Go about your business and let it happen. The waiting is our greatest challenge. We generally think something should be happening. Intellectually, we think we know **what** it should be and also **when** it should be!

• The seventh step is to **GIVE THANKS**.

Sustain your conviction by giving thanks that it's already been done. Develop an attitude of gratitude. Giving thanks is a continual reminder that all good comes from the Source.

... Focus The Attention

Learning to concentrate and meditate is hardest for those who need most to control their subconscious minds. For some, the subconscious mind is like a willful child who cannot pay attention for more than a moment before scampering off to enjoy his or her own play devices.

When you implement visual imaging, your time of concentration may not last more than twenty seconds. If so, you need to take more time for daily practice. The time for holding an image can be gradually lengthened. In this way, the subconscious mind is brought to heel. An average time of between one and two minutes for such concentration is more than adequate.

Several years ago, the University of Chicago conducted a fascinating experiment. Students with equal ability to play basketball were divided into three separate groups. Then, they were asked to shoot free throws. The percentage of baskets made by each team was recorded. Next, the students were given some unusual instructions.

The first group was told not to practice or play basketball at all for thirty days.

The second group was told to practice shooting baskets every day for one hour during the next thirty days.

The third group was instructed to stay off the basketball court for thirty days. Instead — for an hour each day — they were to mentally visualize shooting baskets.

At the end of the thirty days, the groups' skills were reassessed. As you would expect, Group One, which hadn't practiced at all, made no improvement over its original score. Group Two, which had practiced diligently, improved its performance by twenty-four percent.

The most marked results were found, however, in Group Three. This group, which imaged shooting baskets instead of practicing on the basketball court, improved its performance by a phenomenal twenty-three percent! An improvement that was nearly as great as the group that actually practiced on the court each day.

The reason? If there is one secret to the operation of the

subconscious mind, it is that it cannot tell the difference between a real experience and one that is vividly imagined. It is medically and scientifically recognized that visualized images bring about psychological and physiological changes to virtually the same degree as a direct experience.

Affirm the finished product. Beware of the trap of defining the means by which your affirmation is fulfilled. Don't affirm a certain amount of money for your car. After all, the car is your desire, not the amount of money it takes to purchase the car. By affirming the means, you limit the channel through which your car is manifested. Instead, your affirmation might sound something like: "I believe the all-powerful Source is bringing this car to me now. If not this car, then something better."

Keys to the Kingdom

We are mind beings. We don't, as I've said, live in our houses, our cities, or our states. Rather we live in our minds. Everything starts with thought. We are the managers of our own minds and responsible for the thought choices we make. Our challenge is to keep our conscious mind thinking positive and aligning it with a belief system that is also positive.

You are in charge of your decisions, your choices, your ultimate fate. The initiative to take charge of your life is yours for the taking. You have a responsibility to make of your life what you can. You are the supreme ruler of your own personal kingdom!

(1) **"The Man Who Thinks He Can"** by Walter D. Wintle, From **Poems That Live Forever**, Selected by Hazel Fellman, Doubleday & Co., Inc. New York, 1965, P-310

(2) Maxwell Maltz, ***Psycho-Cybernetics*** (Prentice-Hall, Inc., 1960)

(3) Charles Fillmore, **Twelve Powers of Man** (Unity Village, MO., Unity School of Christianity, 1930)

Chapter Three

The Ultimate Determiner Of Your Success

"I went to Europe to find myself, but I wasn't there."

Anonymous

It may come as a surprise, but how you feel about yourself — your self-esteem — is the greatest force in your life. It determines everything about you: your job, your financial condition, your emotional and physical well-being, your social status, your relationships, and even the neighborhood where you live. On occasion, virtually all of us have had to combat negative self-esteem. A poor self-image can make it almost impossible to get ahead in life. No matter how much ability and potential you have, and no matter how hard you try, happiness and fulfillment remain just beyond your reach.

The Power of Your Self-Image

Maxwell Maltz, the world-renowned plastic surgeon, wrote in his book, **Psycho-Cybernetics**[1]:

The self-image is key to human personality and human behavior. Change the self-image and you change the personality and behavior. But more than this. The self-image sets the boundaries of individual accomplishment. It defines what you can and cannot be. Expand the self-image and you expand the area of the possible. The development of an adequately realistic self-image will seem to imbue the individual with new capabilities, new talents, and literally turn failure into success.

Your self-image is so important that one study after another concludes that your view of yourself is the key factor in regulating your life.

The best news is that you can change your self-image.

People fail to succeed, not because they are incapable of success, but because of a failed perception of themselves. Negative, preconceived beliefs and expectations build up resistance. People become convinced ahead of time that it is impossible for them, with their "limited" capacities, to succeed. Once we attach emotion to this belief, logic and reason do little to change it.

For example, Edna, a woman of Mexican ancestry in her mid-fifties, had never learned to read or write. She had taken three different courses within a five-year period to accomplish her one dream of being able to read and write. But her poor self-image persisted: "I'm not smart enough to learn. It's too hard for me." This perception fights to keep her from achieving her goal. To date, it has. After the three unsuccessful attempts, she was on her way to convincing herself of its accuracy.

It is not your ability, but your belief about your ability that holds the controlling interest in determining whether you will or will not succeed.

Imagine the devastating cost in Edna's life of such a negative self-image.

What We Expect, We Get

Perhaps a better gauge than any test devised of how well a person will perform at work or in school is the person's self-image. Because my background is in the field of education, I'm familiar with the research on the relationship of school achievement and self-image. Ask any kindergarten teacher and she'll tell you that she can spot the "believers" and "non-believers" after a few days in the classroom.

Fortunately, a self-image can be changed. However, it presents a real challenge in an educational setting where a certain percentage of students is expected to fail. It would be interesting if educators, instead of giving remedial training in a particular subject, presented strategies to create positive attitudes. This attitude would be reflected in beliefs such as, "I can learn" or, "I will learn."

Teachers

Many are familiar with a study in which two teachers were each given a group of students. One group was "advanced"; the other, "slow." However, the teachers were not told which students belonged to which group. One teacher was told that hers were the brighter students, when, in fact, she had the slow learners. The other was given the slow students, and, conversely, was told she would instruct the group of brighter students.

You guessed it! What the teachers expected is exactly what they got! The slow students were expected to perform, and so they made tremendous progress. But the brighter students, of whom little was expected, did poorly.

Two special points need to be made. First, we live up to the expectations others have of us. Secondly, we can change our perception of ourselves and, thus, greatly impact our performance. What we believe about ourselves is most often an opinion, not a fact.

Believers

We perform better in the presence of a "believer." Did you ever have a boss or supervisor who didn't believe in you or belittled your abilities? Everything you did, was received negatively. What happened? You probably began to feel incompetent and unworthy.

A friend of mine experienced this phenomenon. Her work performance was highly praised by her manager. But suddenly, a new office manager had only criticism for her efforts. She began to believe the worst, and watched her self-image dwindle to almost nothing in less than a week. Fortunately, she found other employment before she became an emotional believer of the negative.

Conversely, we have all worked under managers who enthusiastically encouraged us and recognized our contributions. Because of their belief in our abilities, we performed more productively than ever before. Remember, this is the same you who received negative feedback previously!

Have You Ever Said...?

What follows is a listing of powerful self-image statements which help to determine our success or failure. Recognize any of them?

- I could never speak in front of a group.

- I'm not smart enough to go to college.

- I have trouble making decisions.

- I could never be a salesperson. I don't have what it takes.

- I'm not a risk-taker. I like to play it safe.

- I was just born this way. I can't help myself.

- I have no will power.

- I'm a $20,000 a year person.

- I'm just a housewife. I have no marketable skills.

- I'll never find a mate.

- I can't pass up the cookies.

- I can't take any pressure on the job. I always get migraines.

- I'm just an average student.

- I've gone as far as I can go.

- I'm too old to try.

Each statement is a mirror reflection of a person's self-image.

Each statement is not a fact. It's an opinion belonging to you or someone else. However, the subconscious mind treats the opinion as fact.

Each statement limits your life.

Desire Gets Results

Remember the first time you tried to ride a bicycle? I remember it well. I wobbled around and, in order to stop, ran into a neighbor's car. It would have been easy at that moment to never ride again. (I might add that the neighbor rather hoped I wouldn't!)

Perhaps, you better recall the first time you got behind the wheel of a car and attempted to aim it in the right direction. You were probably tense. Perhaps your nervousness caused you to panic and quickly slam on the brakes, a mistake that almost propelled you through the windshield. (Personally, I think my instructor could have sued me for whiplash!) These experiences could have shattered us and left us proclaiming, "I'll never learn how to do something as tough as driving a car." Perhaps because the desire was so strong, you forged ahead with a new image and envisioned your ultimate success.

I can personally respond to the statement, "I could never speak in front of a group." It's hard to believe now that public speaking is the way I make my living. In college, I saved all the required speech courses until the last semester before graduation. I would get physically ill when facing an audience of any size!

When I was a financially destitute graduate student, the dean of the college approached me one day. "I can give you an assistantship if you'll teach a course in Introductory Psychology," he said. Financial considerations and my desperate need to stay in school outweighed my fear. I began to teach.

What followed was a change in self-image and thus a change in my career path. I went on to become a college level instructor after graduation. I continued in this capacity for 10 years!

Now, I travel and give seminars and workshops full time. Had I been asked twenty years ago if I would get up in front of a classroom or a group of five thousand professionals, I would have responded, "Never! I couldn't do that."

I Want to be Somebody to Somebody

Contrary to what many of us believe, people aren't born with a negative self-image. It is acquired through the conditioning of a failure to gain approval as children. We all grow up with one important need in our lives: we need approval and love from our significant others, particularly our parents.

The methods we used to get this approval as children become the methods by which we seek emotional satisfaction for the rest of our lives. This often leaves individuals living on an emotional roller coaster. They strive to improve their self-esteem through outer performances or approval from others.

Finding Our Roots

After I ask people how they sought approval as children, the next question I ask is the manner in which that approval was given. I ask **how** they received approval. Was it verbal reinforcement? Was it emotional reinforcement such as touching, telling, or demonstrating in some way that they were okay?

The means by which approval is given is frequently very important to us. As we mature, it's how we give our acceptance to others. In other words, if you received lots of verbal reinforcement as a child, you are today probably a very good provider of verbal reinforcement to those around you. It seems to be an automatic function, because it is, after all, in the emotional computer of your mind.

We can identify some of the conditions that occur regularly in the lives of many by asking, "How did you get approval as a child from your parents?" The answer to this all-important question is an emotional imprint that continues to be a point of reference for the rest of our lives. It serves to justify our feelings about ourselves.

I remember Frank. He came into my office feeling somewhat depressed. He was forty-seven years old, a very successful farmer, and a workaholic.

I'm personally not a believer in ferreting out all the secrets of a person's past to learn in the present and plan for the future. But there is always one area of the past that I investigate. "Tell me about your parents. Which was the easiest to receive nurturing from? Which one was the most difficult to get approval from?"

Whenever I ask an audience, "How many of you had

one parent whose approval was easier to get than the other?" a majority of hands go up. In Frank's case, his mother was a very nurturing and accepting person. It was very difficult, however, for Frank to gain approval from his father.

His parents still lived across the road in the old home place. Frank and his father jointly farmed the land of his childhood.

I asked Frank, "How have you sought your father's approval?"

"Well, I'm an achiever," he answered. "I try to work hard to meet his expectations. I try to set a good example, to be responsible and reliable."

I asked him if these things had worked.

As the tears fell, Frank said, "I believe I got his approval once last fall." (Remember, this man was forty-seven years old. He had worked all his life to achieve this all-important validation.)

I asked him, "What did you do, after forty-seven years, that finally gained your father's approval?"

"Well, I took him for a walk in my soybean field. When we got to the other side, I looked at my father and said, 'You know, I think this is the best crop I've ever raised.'" Then Frank told me he waited and waited for his father's reply. Finally, his dad looked at him and said, "Not half bad."

Frank continues to follow his pattern of seeking, working, and searching. If he ever meets the conditions and receives his father's full approval, he will more than likely be able to acknowledge his true worth. Until that time, however, Frank continues to wait for outside approval in order to feel better about himself.

I have found this particular method of gaining approval to be quite common among eldest children like Frank. They are in the unique position of being models and teachers for the siblings that follow.

It is not uncommon for the oldest child to receive approval for achievements or to gain feedback for accomplishments. In this particular case, I was convinced that Frank's workaholic approach to life was an exaggerated attempt to gain his father's love and acceptance.

A Case for the Defense

Tom was a lawyer in his early forties. He was going through what he described as a mid-life crisis. He struggled with very low self-esteem, even though his career accomplishments were, by any standards, outstanding. He was not fulfilled even though his walls were lined with awards.

I discovered that Tom's father was a well-known, respected lawyer in our state. The expectation was that Tom would follow in his father's footsteps. The tragedy was that the son didn't really like law as a profession. He worked hard to earn all the awards and recognition for one reason only. Tom hoped his father, who officed across the hall, would someday walk in, look at those prestigious accomplishments on the walls, and validate his son as a success.

This scenario still had not taken place. Tom was at a fork in the road of his life. He questioned whether he would continue with law as a profession or if he would completely change his career. I asked him when, in his life, had he felt the best about himself. When was his self-esteem at its highest?

"Oh, that's easy," Tom answered. "When I was in college I majored in Art and Music for a year. Then my father discovered what I was doing. He insisted that I change to law."

Here's just another example of a whole life spent searching for parental approval in a manner that conflicted with the person's unique gifts and talents. He did not feel free to pursue his own interests because of the overwhelming need to please his father.

Now, Tom had to make the decision whether to claim his original birthright or to continue to evaluate himself based on a feeling. An opinion is not a fact. His feelings of inadequacy did not make him inadequate.

Pleasing You Pleases Me

Another condition that arises is that of trying to be a "pleaser" to everyone. A pleaser hopes that approval and acceptance will be achieved through his efforts. Pleasers have a difficult time in life, and rightly so.

If one plays the role of pleaser, it may not bring the hoped-for results from a parent/parents, a co-worker, supervisor, friend or spouse. In the face of this disappointment, the role of a pleaser can be emotionally devastating. It is not unlikely or uncommon that pleasers attach themselves to individuals whom they cannot please, just as they were unable to please a parent as children.

In a recent workshop, I explained the pleaser's search in terms of his or her pain. Pleasers trust others far more than they trust their own feelings. Their search is exhausting and painful.

A woman approached me with tears in her eyes and said, "I wondered all my life why I had such poor self-esteem and why I kept finding myself in relationships that resulted in so much pain. I had parents that I couldn't please. I also married a man that I couldn't please no matter what I did." She added, "Now that I understand the cause for why I feel so badly about myself, it's like being set free."

The biggest challenge for a pleaser is to learn to trust his or her feelings more than trusting others' opinions. Pleasers frequently don't take risks in their lives. Nor do they take advantage of opportunities to enhance their lives. They have to go home and get approval from all their significant others before they do anything.

Invariably, someone shoots down their ideas or opportunities. As a result, they fold up. They give up because the need to please transcends the need to grow.

Let's Call a Truce

Others feel good about themselves by being "peace-makers." These are individuals who grow up being what I call the "harmonizers" in the family. Peacemakers do anything to avoid conflict and confrontation. As a result, they are frequently very charming and easy to be around.

I often find this pattern in the working world. Such individuals are often promoted because they are well-liked, get along easily with others, and avoid rocking the boat or causing conflict. Oftentimes, however, they are promoted into positions of responsibility which require that they make decisions resulting in discomfort for others.

Sally is a peacemaker who was promoted into such a position. Her first assignment was to dismiss another employee in her department. This caused her great emotional upheaval, because she had gone through life avoiding confrontation and conflict. Now she was in a position that involved these very qualities. Way back, as a child, she found recognition by being a harmonizing, peacemaking individual. To do anything other than this brought on feelings of inadequacy and resulted in poor self-esteem.

Putting in Overtime

Hard work is another method for achieving approval. I have asked people about how they gained approval from those around them when they were young. Some will ponder for a moment and then say, "Well, in our family, hard work was the way we gained approval." Others admit, "I'm not sure if we were actually told that hard work was the way to get approval, but we certainly felt it through the expectations placed on us." Hard work, then, becomes the way to achieve emotional satisfaction and, hopefully, a positive feeling of self-esteem.

Sometimes, just being a companion, working side by side with someone, makes a person feel emotionally acceptable. Within marriage, this pattern continues to reflect the same need to feel emotionally loved or accepted by a mate. These people feel emotionally distraught when they are denied opportunities to be a companion or to do things with their mates. This is another example of an early learned pattern of self-acceptance that results in a positive perception of themselves.

Mark, the Menace

Let's take a quick look at the family "trouble maker." I remember Mark. Mark was the younger sibling of a "model child," which is a difficult position at best. Although the feedback he received for pushing to the limits and beyond was negative, it still gained him scads of attention.

This was Mark's intention. His philosophy mandated that "rules were meant to be broken" and that "limits were set as starting points for experimentation."

Even in his life today, Mark has difficulty accepting boundaries. His self-identified "free spirit" continues to get him attention in the work place. The calm and peaceful times in his life are cause for re-evaluation, because his self-esteem is tied so closely to his ability to cause a disturbance or to do something rather unusual.

If You Don't Hear From Me...

Oftentimes, individuals can't recall exactly what it was they did that gained them feedback and acceptance. But one of the common responses I get is, "no news is good news."

In other words, when these people did things that were accepted or expected, they heard nothing. But when mistakes were made, they heard plenty! These individuals grew up taking charge of their lives until someone stopped them. Until this happened, they felt positive about their self-esteem and very negative whenever they strayed from those limits of acceptance.

Group Dynamics

When people are teamed together in a working environment, these emotional methods for self-acceptance certainly do stand out. Can you imagine the dynamics between a person programmed with "no news is good news" and a secretary who is a pleaser? The pleaser works ninety-nine days straight, trying his or her best to please the boss.

On the hundredth day, a mistake is made. Until that time, the secretary received no feedback about the ninety-nine days of good hard work. However, on the hundredth day, the day of the mistake, the roof fell in.

It seems that all of us use whatever method makes us feel good about ourselves. The methods we learned early on become our emotional check points for self-esteem.

No Substitutions Please

The real tragedy is when individuals **never** receive approval. They have **no** emotional point of reference to determine when they have succeeded. They live their whole lives with low self-esteem because they rely on their feelings rather than on the fact of their basic, inherent self-worth.

It's not uncommon for a difficult parent to die without the child ever receiving the parent's approval. In that event, they continue the struggle to come to terms with the loss and to be at peace with it.

Nothing else seems to satisfy or fill the emotional void left by an inability to gain the acceptance of that parent. Even a mate cannot take the place of this original source of self-esteem.

A gentleman in his late sixties once came up to me at the end of a seminar I conducted. "I have to share something with you," this man said to me. "I have always taken a back seat to my wife's efforts to please a mother who always criticized her. I have often felt left out. But now I understand her emotional need to pursue this. The tragedy though is that it will probably never be accomplished. My total acceptance of her has never replaced what she doesn't get from her mother."

Role or Real?

As I said, one of the most popular ways to keep our self-esteem manageable is to seek the approval of others. The way we do this reflects the way we learned as children. We continue to do it and often spend our whole lives in emotional pain pursuing what continues to elude us.

Perhaps unfulfilled needs for self-esteem underlie every human act, both positive and negative.

In the course of your lifetime, you will no doubt wear the "hat" or "mask" of thirty-five to fifty different roles. Every role has a set of expectations. The importance of these roles and how you fulfill them depends on your inner core, your self-esteem. The roles closest to the core are of greater importance. You will have more to lose and/or more to gain. Likewise, they will consume most of your thoughts, energy, and time.

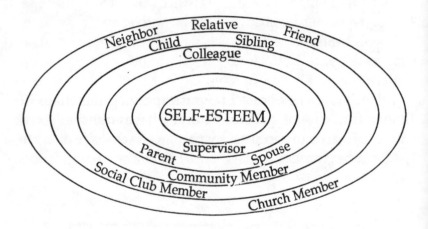

Self Worth...It Was There All the Time

Self-esteem is the human hunger for approval. But I believe you were given freedom from this life-long quest for approval that seeks to justify your existence. This freedom comes in the form of a gift. It is a gift that arises from the Source, the gift of your self-worth. I call self-worth the human hunger for divine acceptance. It's your inheritance — given to all equally — and it's yours for the claiming. It has nothing to do with opinion or feeling because it just simply is a fact. I am somebody.

I believe we are spiritually designed to enjoy the position and privilege befitting a child of God. Simply, we were created to go first class, to live and give only that which reflects dignity, both human and divine. If we lose our awareness of this dignity, we risk becoming as the animals in the jungle.

It's a Gift

I'm taking the liberty of oversimplifying this magnificent gift. (I'm sure you won't mind.) It was given to you at birth. Everyone received exactly the same gift at birth, regardless of race, parentage, background, or circumstances. It is what I call the:

Unconditional Acceptance

It is the divine gift of self-worth. This "pound" entitles you to take every course that will enable you to grow and to fulfill the true mission of your life. It has unlimited talents, dreams, ideas, and potential within it. All of these await your discovery. We were meant to grow and develop into the beings we were designed to be, each of us using what was uniquely given to us.

This pound of worth entitles us to experience ourselves in this growth-enhancing process. While we are experiencing — taking classes, if you will — at this earthly university, there is no failure. It's all knowledge for the purpose of growth.

This pound of worth is given to us regardless of our parentage and whether or not we achieved approval. It is given to us independent of our cultural background, our race, color, or any other circumstance that might cause us to be less than another or less than we were meant to be.

It's Changeless

When we graduate from the University of Earth, we will have the same pound of self-worth. It is our birthright and our inheritance. On the journey through life, no one can add one ounce to this pound of worth. Nor can anyone or any circumstance subtract from it.

It is a fact of your true existence that you have inside of you all that you can be. What we fail to realize is that this gift is a fact. It's not just a feeling or an opinion. Why is it then that our self-esteem — which is not the same as our self-worth — does not reflect this marvelous gift with all its entitlements?

It's Yours for the Taking

As a result of claiming this gift, we should know that we are unique, entitled, and privileged. But often we do not understand this. Instead, we listen to others' comments and interpret today's experiences based on past events. These interpretations become lodged in our mind computers. They often generate strong beliefs and feelings that we are less than adequate.

In other words, we look at this beautiful pound of worth through the eyes of distorted emotions. We conclude that we are somewhere between the full weight of that worth and the smallest degree measurable. We look at our worth as if it were just a half of a pound and say to ourselves, "I don't have as much worth as so-and-so." The moment you declare yourself to be less than you actually are, your self-esteem responds accordingly.

Feeling or Fact?

Back to self-esteem and your distorted perception of your pound of worth. It is a **feeling**. Your worth is a **fact**.

A desire for the good feelings associated with positive self-esteem drives us to seek recognition and approval through external accomplishments. Your self-esteem becomes dependent on others rather than dependent on the true Source of your original gift.

Our life-long quest begins then when we attempt to keep our self-esteem manageable and at a tolerable level. We look at the conditions we have always tried to meet and the people we've always tried to please in order to feel good about ourselves.

How do you know whether or not a person has claimed his worth? How do you know if he's living a life based upon feelings about himself? Perhaps, one of the easiest ways is to give the person a compliment. If the compliment is accepted graciously, with thanks given back, you can be fairly certain that the person knows the fact of his self-worth. A great many people, however, attempt to discount the compliment.

Perhaps you just told someone that he looks nice today. The person denies it! He may either try to justify what he has on, or he may actually criticize it. It becomes apparent that the person feels uncomfortable acknowledging any good that comes from external sources. Some days, we feel like half an ounce! Something might happen that sends that feeling down to its lowest depths. But we have to keep reminding ourselves, with healthy self-talk, that we were born with as much worth as anybody else. We need to claim and act upon this natural birthright.

Unfortunately, many of us have not internalized this. We still struggle with a limited emotional perception, which depends on outside circumstances, in hopes of feeling better inside. Of course, external conditions only reflect inner belief systems. The cause is inside...the results or the circumstances are outside. We live our lives from inside out.

But, I Only Received 1/2 a Pound!

How can we find the missing piece? If we can find it, if

we can earn it in some manner, then we will be justified in claiming our true worth.

Chances are that the means by which we sought approval as children will be the same method we fall back on today when seeking approval from others. If being compliant or rebellious, if being a peace-maker, a pleaser, or an achiever worked for you, then it's natural that you will start with this familiar approach, an approach that paid dividends before.

If you didn't get approval from your significant others as a child, your methodology might be a case of trial and error. Often this leaves you emotionally at a loss because you don't know what it feels like to receive unconditional love and approval.

Save Me, Save Me!

Another means of "earning" the right to love ourselves is through the relationships we establish. We try to increase our self-worth through marriage, friendships, or relationships with others who we think have more self-esteem than we have.

In other words, if I claim only half of my pound, then I might feel a need to attach myself to someone who I think has claimed his/her full pound. In this way, I try to enhance my self-esteem. This approach is fraught with pain and disillusionment because each of us has the same amount of worth.

Our self-worth cannot be added to or subtracted from through any relationship we develop. Still, we continue to try to enhance our self-esteem by being seen with or associating with these "pound-plussers." We think such associations increase our worth.

What we attach our self-esteem to controls us. To depend on others for good feelings about ourselves places us in bondage to these people. True slavery and unrelenting bondage result if we allow others to control our lives.

I have noticed over time that those who claim their birthright and their pound of worth tend to seek and attract those of like poundage. Like attracts like. We are most comfortable with those most like ourselves.

Meet My Other Half

I've also noticed that those who only claim half or even a quarter of their pound migrate to others who have claimed a like amount. These "halfers" think they make a whole pound when joined together; the "quarter-pounders" join together and limp along feeling unfulfilled and unacceptable to themselves! If you are in bondage to your other half, then you are controlled by it.

The truth is that we are all whole beings and we share this wholeness with others. We don't need anyone else to provide us with our missing parts.

Actions Speak Louder

Those who feel inadequate and have low self-esteem tend to do abusive things to others in order to feel better and superior about themselves. In fact, how we treat others is a reflection of how we view ourselves. The lower our self-esteem, the more difficult we are in our relationships with others. (However, some individuals withdraw into themselves rather than lashing out at others.)

People who love themselves claim their natural birthright pound of worth. They treat others with the same respect they expect for themselves.

If you don't recall exactly what means you utilized to achieve approval as a child, or if you never did receive it, the next question is to ask: "What gives me a feeling of emotional satisfaction?" That is, what makes you feel good or at least better about yourself? There are some individuals who can't answer this question at all.

But for many there is something outside of themselves that often triggers an emotional okay-ness. Whatever this force is, it becomes your method for achieving good feelings about yourself. It may also become your bondage as well.

"I'll Get to the Top and Prove It!"

Many people try to enhance their self-worth through achievements. The work ethic becomes their "worth ethic." Material things of course do not build permanent self-esteem. Self-worth that is rooted in materialistic status symbols (money, power, position, etc.), has a short life span.

When I'm a Size Eight and My Nose is Straight

There is another method — certainly a product of the

western world — whereby we measure our self-esteem by the way we look. People who don't reflect the image portrayed by major advertisers often have poor self-esteem and feel inadequate.

From what many of us have learned about the futility of dieting, we know we must first love ourselves as we are and claim our true worth. Then we can decide whether we want to lose those extra pounds or love ourselves in spite of them. Think for a moment of how much time and energy we squander in pursuit of external forces with which we measure our self-esteem. This squandered time and energy is beyond measure and results in much pain.

Only When I Reach Perfection

On a personal note, I have also waged a battle with my self-esteem as I've journeyed through life. My mother is a perfectionist, particularly in the area of housekeeping responsibilities. She feels, even in these later years of her life, that her self-esteem is based on her home and how it looks. When it looks to her satisfaction, then emotionally she feels good about herself.

... Making the Grade

My childhood was controlled by the house I lived in. If it was dirty (not that I remember it ever was!), then we couldn't have company over because it didn't look right. If the house was cleaned up, we had to be careful with company so that it wouldn't get messed up. It was kind of a Catch-22.

It was difficult for me to do things around the house that met with my mother's satisfaction. There was always room for further improvement! In truth, there probably **was** room for improvement, but in my emotional perception, it appeared that I never passed the test.

I remember the frustration of trying to make a bed properly. (One day, I even got out a paper and pencil to list the many ways there were to correctly make a bed. There aren't that many!) After I finished making my bed, I always waited for my mother. Sooner or later, she came into my room and gave my bed her one-more-fluff (the term I used to describe her smoothing action), and then all was well. Unfortunately, those one-more-fluffs erased any good I felt for all my efforts.

As a girl, I decided there was no way I would ever win this war. But someday, I would have my own house and I would live in it and enjoy it. I would not be compulsively controlled by how it looked.

. . . Here Come 'de Judge

This is exactly what I did. I was doing quite well and feeling okay about myself. Then my mother would come to visit. As I prepared for her arrival, I watched my self-esteem dwindle down to half an ounce.

I felt inadequate because the priorities in my life were not the same as those in her life. Before her arrival, it took all my energy to keep that half-ounce feeling from totally destroying me. As I said earlier, where your mind goes, your energy flows. I was physically drained by the time she arrived.

I tried to compensate for my low self-esteem and feelings of inadequacy. The conscious mind is a very cagey operator. On these occasions, it served me well as the rescuer of my emotions. Our conscious minds are able to keep low self-esteem from destroying us through their many strategies.

For instance, our conscious minds rationalize for us and procrastinate. This was certainly true in my case, as I began to take an inventory of my house. I thought to myself, "Uh-oh, I'd better get this ready for inspection." I thought my mother was coming to do just that! This couldn't have been further from the truth. But when our self-esteem is low, we begin to experience paranoia. We make assumptions that aren't true at all.

. . . Clutter's Last Stand

The first thing I would do was check the bathroom linen closet. My towels were haphazardly stuffed in the shelves. I told myself that I had to straighten them up because "that's not the way I was raised."

My conscious mind argued otherwise: "Don't worry about it. The only person who would stack towels in color coordinated little piles behind the closed doors of a bathroom, must mean to sell them. Since you're not going to sell your towels, don't bother to straighten them up." (Now, that's the kind of rationalizing your conscious mind is capable of as it deals with information coming from your five senses.)

I said to myself: "Dresser drawers! They're a mess." I just knew that somebody would pull one out and there it would be, a disgusting example of poor housekeeping!

My conscious mind rescued me once again: "Don't worry about the drawers either. Anyone who needs something from a dresser drawer ought to have to work to find it. Don't make it easy and just lay it right out."

But then I remembered the dirt behind the TV! I didn't crawl back there too often. But I knew there were probably quite a few fuzzies lurking there.

My conscious mind piped right in: "Now, that's the easiest of all. Anyone who crawls behind a corner TV deserves what he gets. He ought to get dirty. No one has any business back there unless he's a repairman. And, if that's the case, too bad. He's getting paid to be back there!" (That's where the mind and your energy go. It's trying to rationalize away the half-ounce feeling.)

By the way, in my frustration at knowing that I probably couldn't pass inspection, I took my low self-esteem out on my children. You see, I thought my mother was going to walk through my front door and say, "Oh, where did I go wrong?"

This was not the case at all. This was my distorted perception due to a low self-esteem in this particular area of housekeeping. This pattern continued for years. Every anticipated visit of my mother caused an emotional trauma because of my emotional self-evaluation.

Finally, several years ago, I took a good look at this situation. "I must do something about this," I said. "Mother's visits are so precious and special. But every visit is preceded by self-inflicted trauma, because I feel that I have disappointed her." I asked myself what I could do to make these visits less traumatizing for me. I decided that I had the same three options I gave you!

1. **Change my mother.** This is a bit ridiculous because my mother still has her self-esteem tied to her house. It's a vital part of her self-evaluation. So, I'm not going to change her.

2. **Change the environment or the situation.** I could either move before she arrives or I could put her in a hotel. Those options are out as they are neither practical nor desirable.

3. **Change myself.** I could make the situation more pleasant by doing something about myself. What could I do? I could change my mind or my attitude about this. I could give up feeling emotionally devastated by every visit.

   Or I could change my behavior by cleaning the house superbly, by hiring someone else to do it, or by acting upon this situation in some other way.

Within this third option, I chose to change my attitude. As I pondered this problem while driving one day, a light bulb went on. It dawned on me that people who are compulsive and chase after things — just like my mother chased after dirt — do so because they enjoy what they're chasing. They like the results of what they're chasing.

Up until this time, I thought my mother chased dirt because she **didn't** like it. However, it occurred to me that my mother might really **like** dirt. I decided to save mine for her!

. . . I've Got it "Maid"

I'll never forget her first visit after this revelation. "Now mother," I said to her, "if you get bored while I'm at work tomorrow, I have something saved for you. All sorts of lint, dirt, and dust. You can do as you please with it!"

I'll never forget her response. "I've been waiting all these years to do something helpful for you. But I would never touch your house without your permission."

Can you believe that I missed out on years and years of free housecleaning? Just because I thought my house was the measurement of my self-esteem, I missed a golden opportunity. Now, here's my mother asking me what time I leave for work because she's hoping to get an early start!

Recently she told me that her health was not what it had been. It wasn't easy for her to clean my entire house anymore. "That's all right, mother," I said, "you'll just have to do it in stages and come more often. This is your job!"

Perfection is a total illusion. To attempt to make any

aspect of our lives perfect so we can feel good about ourselves is like the cat which chases after its tail.

Give What You Wanted to Get

Many of us have steadfastly sought approval and possibly never received it. But some of us reach a point where we overcome this lack and decide to give approval to significant others, instead of waiting for them to give it first.

Used Clothing

It has been my experience that those who have not received approval from their parents also have grandparents who didn't give approval to their children. We give to others that which was given to us. This pattern remains fixed unless we consciously consider the effects and choose to change those hand-me-downs that are not favorable.

Bridging the Gap

I remember a fellow who attended one of my workshops. His name was Doug. He had become aware of his own search for this elusive emotional satisfaction from his father.

"I made up my mind that it was time to confront this issue," Doug told me. "I spent too many years being fearful and uncomfortable around my father. I always felt I was not what he wanted me to be. I just didn't quite measure up in some way."

One summer, when his dad came to visit, Doug watched his father out trimming the bushes. He thought to himself, "Now's the time." He went out to the front yard and approached his father. "Dad, I need to talk to you," Doug said. "For so many years I've wondered if you were satisfied with me, or if I disappointed you in some way. I've never really felt that I had your acceptance. I just want you to know that I love you and that I realize it's time for me to deal with this. I don't want to hurt you, but this is very important to me. I really want to please you."

His father, with tears rolling down his cheeks, turned to him and said, "Son, I couldn't be more proud of you. I guess I'm not very good at expressing it. You see, I never heard it from my parents, and I always wondered if I had satisfied them." Through their tears, the two men embraced on the front lawn.

Doug told me, "I'm happy to say now that we are the very best of friends. We call each other often and chat as friends chat. I'm so grateful this bridge was crossed, because I never had such talks with my father before."

Speak Out and Touch Someone

I also recall another man who sat in the front row at one of my workshops. I challenged my audience to confront those people in their lives who needed to hear, "I love you," "I'm proud of you," or whatever else might be a way to express approval. I further encouraged them to do so before the sun went down that night. It would truly change a life. An all-consuming search could end. True self-worth could be claimed. And a person would be free to pursue their interests and dreams with full use of their talents.

I received a letter from this gentleman in the front row. He had accepted my challenge.

"I went to the telephone that night and called my thirty-two year old son," he wrote. "I had always been very tough on that boy. It was very difficult for him to please me. I never really gave him any feedback as to whether or not he did, but I gave him loads of criticism.

"I said to him: 'Son, I'm long overdue and I hope that I'm not too late. I just want you to know that I love you and I couldn't be prouder of you as my son.'

"My son broke down and cried and I'm sure that Ma Bell raked in the money that night as we talked and wept for what seemed like hours. I'll never forget his comment before we hung up. He said, 'Thank you, Dad. Now I can get on with the rest of my life.'"

The "Open Hand" Policy

I have a little exercise which I implement in some of my seminars. You might want to try it.

Open your right hand, Mentally put in this hand all of the circumstances and things you don't wish to lose: relationships, ideas, traditions, money, the office (with the window), your collections, your expectations. You get the idea? Now, close your right hand tightly and make a fist.

Then, open your left hand. Put in this hand all your worries, doubts, fears, and anxieties, every feeling associated with the potential loss of those things in your right hand. Make a fist with your left hand.

The first thing you notice is the body's response to these tightly closed fists. Your body becomes tense and rigid. For everything you have inside those fists is your ceiling. Nothing new can enter your life. Innovative ideas and magnificent opportunities go unrecognized. Also, everything in those clenched fists will ultimately be lost. The only questions are "how" and "when." All that you accumulate externally will be left behind when you graduate.

Life is to be lived with an open hand. Loosen those white-knuckled fists. You first notice your physical response. It's one of relief and relaxation. Loosely cup your right hand and add all those previously held commodities back into its relaxed palm.

Everything is on loan to you to pass on to others. With an open hand, there is no need to nurture fear, worry or to feel anxiety. The open hand makes room for more when something leaves. The laws of nature cannot tolerate a vacuum and so there will not be one.

Can you remember ever watching a child pick up a baby bird for the first time? (Perhaps you did this yourself.) The child's first instinct is to squeeze the little body to ensure its captivity. "Oh, no," we warn the child. "Be careful. You'll kill it if you hold it too tightly." The bird must be free to leave and to live.

One of life's most profound lessons is that what is held

too tightly dies. What is held loosely lives and is free.

Hard work, achievement and position: these are the western world's measurements of success. The real question is the motivation for that drive and ambition. If these are to influence your self-esteem, my concern is, "What happens to your self-esteem when the driving ambition dies out?"

I am Somebody

It doesn't really matter if we've been approved or loved by our significant others. It's the frosting, when we receive this approval. The cake of our life is what we have going for us, in us.

Once you claim your full pound of True Worth, you can immediately get off the emotional roller coaster. When you do get external approval and applause, it truly is the frosting. It's the quiet reassurance and the peace within you that results from acknowledgement of your true worth. It sustains you when external rewards are temporarily at a standstill.

The next time someone pays you a compliment, saying, "My, you look nice!" or "Gee, you did a great job!" you can smile and say, "Thank you." That's what pounders say to others' perceptions of them. While you're enjoying that wonderful, peaceful feeling you can whisper under your breath, "You have excellent taste."

Self-worth is a fact. Once you acknowledge and claim this fact, the feelings never cease to be positive, peaceful and even exhilarating.

If you search for these feelings from an external source, you remain in a state of turmoil, anxiety and even pain. You depend on sources over which you have no control.

Look in the mirror tomorrow morning. Say to that person looking back at you, "YOU made me this way and I am satisfied!"

Whether you're young or old,
   You are Somebody.

Whether you're educated or uneducated,
   You are Somebody.

Whether you're black or white,
   You are Somebody.

Whether you're rich or poor,
   You are Somebody.

Whether you're fat or thin,
   You are Somebody.

Whether you're married or divorced,
   You are Somebody.

Whether you're successful or unsuccessful,
   You are Somebody.

If you feel like 1/2 an ounce, claim your pound...
   You are Somebody.

(1) Maxwell Maltz, **Psycho-Cybernetics**
(Prentice-Hall, Inc., 1960)

Chapter Four

Tapping the Well

Love is a force. It is not a result; it is a cause. It is not a product; it produces. It is a power, like money, or steam or electricity. It is valueless unless you can give something else by means of it.

Anne Morrow Lindbergh

Keeping the Channel Open

So many times, I hear people say they have no control over their feelings. They immediately say whatever is on their minds. To justify an unkindness resulting from such an outburst, these people often use the excuse that they are only "being honest." They are often torn within by raging conflicts brought on by powerful feelings of fear, jealousy, resentment or grief. Sadly, these conflicts hold them in bondage.

When I talk with such people, I often note that they are emotional "wrecks." They are either awash in a river of tears or they lash out blindly with comments such as, "I can't help the way I feel; I have to be honest."

Sometimes I doubt this professed "honesty" and its implication of helplessness. It's difficult when we feel out of control to regain control. It's necessary to realize that we do choose our thoughts and the emotions we buy into.

Clogging Factor I - Fear

The subconscious mind, the center of emotion, houses imprints of past experiences. These prior events are manifested as feelings. Since we are the "choice-makers" of our futures, these feelings become guides to those choices. Feelings direct us in ways that help us meet and manipulate our environments. They are all-purposeful and make sense to us. Some feelings warn us of impending dangers, and thus, we need them for our survival. Others warn us of a malfunction. Still others give meaning to our lives. And some feelings effectively block the good, which waits within the Source, to impact our lives.

The Eternal Bogeyman

Fear is of immeasurable value to us. It can protect our lives. But it can also devastate them. Until we can manage a more reasonable handling of the cause of the crippling force of fear and the teachings about what to do with it, our lives will be haunted by extreme distress and poor health. We need to learn the art of turning our primitive fear into civilized action.

You cannot live well unless you live courageously. Complete safety is only to be achieved through cowardice. The drive to be secure keeps us bound, gagged, and in chains.

. . . A Compelling Force

Fear compels us all to do things we should not do; it makes us afraid to do the things we should. It is like having monkeys on our backs which go to sleep with us in the evening and kick us awake in the morning.

This urge for security and safety can also breed dishonesty. History shows us that peace often brings corruption. But a fearful war may resurrect social harmony. (These wars might have been averted had more individuals maintained a proper focus.) The fact that many heroic deeds are undertaken by soldiers, who themselves are paralyzed by fear, gives credence to this phenomenon.

We've all heard stories of individuals empowered with superhuman strength when faced with a crisis. For example, people who lifted cars from the bodies of loved ones.

The same heroism occurs daily among people who appear too fragile and sheltered to venture forward in a time of adversity. Sally was one of these gentle souls who never knew true hardship. Since birth, she had been coddled and catered to by her family. She was enthroned as an infant, spoiled as a child, and thus formed into a weak woman who had no preparation for the pressures of the real world.

One day, tragedy struck. Sally's husband and only child were killed by a drunken driver. Deep within her soul, something changed. She began to view her own protected and selfish existence with a certain detachment. She was able to focus her energies on others who had experienced similar pain. She came out of herself and became an active participant in an outreach program. Some called it a miracle.

What is this miracle that changes destructive self-protection into constructive action? It is a change of attention away from ourselves and towards others. Remember, whatever your mind attends to is magnified.

Fear is negative imagery projected into the future. Fear is the dread of consequences that might result from a failure to master an event. It's as if you got up in the morning and took this one-of-a-kind, unique life of yours and plugged it into a negative socket. You add the film and then project onto the screen of your mind all the negative thoughts that you can possibly think of and the pictures to accompany them.

... Join the Human Race

There are some fears common to all of us. At one time or another, we all experienced a fear of disapproval, criticism or of losing someone's love. Many of us are afraid to express anger for fear of losing the love and acceptance of others. (However, if you lose their love through expression of your feelings, then you either didn't have it to begin with or it wasn't worth having anyway!)

It isn't hard to imagine that if you made a certain decision, tried something new or made a mistake, that you would meet with strong disapproval and criticism. The people who care about you might not accept you as human and imperfect. The risk of rejection seems a dangerous one. In order to protect yourself, you withdraw and don't make decisions or take risks.

A child experiences no greater fear than that of being abandoned or unloved by his parents. He desperately fears being ignored and rejected. In fact, children derive their sense of identity solely from being loved, cared for, noticed, and approved of.

We never outgrow this need for love and approval. The degrees that are awarded and the honors that are bestowed are only adult counterparts to the fulfillment of this same childhood need. We search for it, hunger for it, and are often damaged if denied it. We are "tin-cuppers," waiting for someone to fill our cups with approval. Denied it, we suffer at a deeper level.

Many people are motivated by a fear of some kind. Common fears include being hurt, growing old, losing a loved one, divorce, poverty, loneliness, pain, rejection, or failure.

... I'll Never be Able to Do It!

The fear of failure is a mind-set that has the potential to paralyze. You imagine that anything you actively strive for and fail to achieve would be an overwhelming personal defeat. Therefore, you refuse to try at all. Our purpose, if you'll remember, is to learn and grow. No one can fail at everything and we all will fail at something.

We have our share of victories and defeats, and certainly it is true that our victories and little "graduations" are very sweet and the difficult times are very bitter. The bad taste, though, will not linger forever when we understand that it is all knowledge.

In order to attain knowledge, we all must continue to reach out and extend ourselves beyond the comfort zones that we've become accustomed to. Within every disappointment, heartbreak, or failure, there exists an equal (and usually greater) positive benefit.

I have a friend who has so effectively programmed his mind to believe this that whenever anything adverse occurs, he immediately looks for the benefit within. What a joy! He often reflects back on all the positive benefits that came into his life as a result of something that first appeared quite negative.

Abraham Lincoln, as you might have heard, failed about nine times in his choice of careers before he finally became president. Each failure was a blessing or opportunity in disguise. The failure directed him onward and upward along his path of learning and growth. Each so-called failure changed the course of his life just enough to prepare him for the next step.

. . . I'll Never be Able to Keep It Up!

Interestingly enough, a fear of success can be as paralyzing to some as the fear of failure is to others. Sometimes, because of a lack of confidence, success seems even more risky than not succeeding. The person is convinced that success is rooted in chance. This is exactly the situation that Steve found himself in during his college experiences. If you'll recall, he had difficulty justifying his success with his belief system. He rationalized away success as being "just luck."

For some, there is a fear that a success pattern will become expected of them, and they won't be able to keep it up. What they ultimately fear is the awful "truth" that they are losers. The fear is that this will be revealed. Since these people are sure that they will eventually fall off the mountain, it seems safer not to climb the mountain at all.

Sometimes, fear of success is seen most often in people who are eldest children. They perceive the expectations of others to be far beyond what they feel they're capable of accomplishing. Perhaps they are convinced that they can't meet or maintain such high standards. They often find themselves not attempting things or actually sabotaging their own efforts. They avoid making any commitment and keep control over their feelings and situations.

. . . I'll Never Have Enough

Greed, lust, envy, jealousy, and gossip are all rooted in fear. The fear is of not having enough of the "good" to go around. This is a "con job" of an ego which always compares or competes with others, forgetting that there is no lack or limitation in the universe.

Jealousy, for example, is the fear that another will get more love than you. If you find yourself comparing or competing, it is because of your own negative thoughts and negative imagery.

Freeing Factor I - Faith

The good news is that this condition of fear can be changed. It can be exchanged for a positive view. In order to replace fearful, negative imagery, refocus your mind's camera on a more positive view. Positive pictures and imagery will result from your conscious efforts to change.

Project those pictures into the future by what is commonly referred to as "faith." When fear drops anchor in the harbor of your life, faith is there to set you free. You must make the choice to either stagnate with fear or to sail with faith. Faith is the substance of things hoped for and the evidence of things not yet seen.

If you'll refer back to the illustration of those things provided to us by the Source, you will see the word "faith." Faith is our mind's ability to perceive the invisible with conviction. It is good.

Believe it or Not

There is an important counterpart to faith, and that is

belief. In the subconscious mind, if you'll recall, our beliefs are programmed. There is a difference between faith and belief. You can believe anything. You can believe in sickness or in health, wealth or poverty, intelligence or ignorance. These beliefs draw you toward whatever you believe in.

Faith, however, never attracts the negative. Belief can involve fear as well as security. But faith never attaches itself to fear. You can find yourself believing in and being drawn to something that is dangerous for you. However, you cannot have faith in something harmful. The gift of faith and your mind's ability to perceive relates only to your good.

Everyone has received this gift of faith. Everyone has the ability to attract good from the invisible, but not everyone does so. Belief is the activator of your faith.

... Only the Worst

Let's suppose you are concerned about whether or not you should make a job change. You hear of an exciting and challenging position opening up. Two of your trusted friends recommend you for the job. It sounds just too good to be true.

As you mull it over, you realize there are a lot of unknowns. You've heard you'll have to be more assertive, and that's a little too risky for you. You don't know the boss. You've heard that she is a real taskmaster and fear you'll probably disappoint her.

The responsibilities are similar to those of your present

position. But you fear there are additional duties that you won't be able to perform. There are opportunities to learn new material and to receive training in other related skills. But you've always had trouble learning new things, and it's been a long time since you were in school.

On the surface, this appears to be the chance of a lifetime. But it could still be the biggest mistake you've ever made. You'll probably just let your friends down and disappoint them immensely.

On the other hand, your present job is a dead-end. It's no longer challenging or fulfilling, and working conditions are awful. Your imagination even comes into play. It creates worse scenarios than your negative thoughts have conjured up so far.

You see yourself being asked to speak before a group. You shake all over. You hear yourself stumbling, mumbling, and embarrassing yourself. Your boss is irritable with you because you have trouble composing a particular letter. She's impatient with your lack of assertiveness. You can't make heads or tails out of your work assignments. There is too little structure, and you don't know what to do or which way to turn. The new skills are impossible to learn. You envision yourself completely paralyzed when face to face with the computer.

You even see that pink slip included with your final paycheck. You knew it would happen. It was just a matter of time! Negative thoughts plus negative imagery equals fear, a lack of belief in yourself.

... Only the Best

Let's change the view. The choice of focus is always up to you. An exciting and new job offer comes your way. Two of your friends who believe strongly in your ability have recommended you for the job. It's not too good to be true. Rather, the job seems perfectly suited to you.

Your present position has left you feeling unmotivated. The new position is just the opportunity you need to help you regain enthusiasm. You have enough familiarity with the job responsibilities to feel confident that the unknowns will only be exciting opportunities. The boss has high expectations and will motivate, challenge, and stretch you. You tell yourself that you need to learn new skills. The opportunity for company-paid training is just about miraculous.

Your friends' confidence in you is confirmed. Instead of the pink slip, you'll be offered a promotion.

Now, your imagination comes into play, creating more exhilarating scenarios than your positive thinking has already conjured up. You see yourself walking into the office dressed for success. You make a presentation to a group and hear yourself successfully fielding all questions. Your boss compliments you on your initiative and competency. She's pleased. You are celebrating your first promotion with your friends. You're mastering the complexities of that computer with ease and confidence.

Positive thoughts plus positive imagery equals a belief in yourself. After all, you deserve it!

Your Attention, Please

Our relationship with life depends on the way we use our attention. If our attention is negative, all the good promised to us from the Source is blocked. If it is positive, all the inner power is released.

Fear can never be overcome by trust in external circumstances or values. These are subject to every phase of destruction. We are freed from anxieties when we learn to depend on inner values of mind and heart. Fear is conquered or made inevitable according to the direction the mind takes. The way you think protects or destroys your life.

You are set free from fear when you turn your attention to the positive good that lies within every situation. This faith is our ability to perceive the invisible good with absolute conviction. Remember, what you perceive and believe, you shall receive. This affirmative attitude is a belief that constructive ways of life are available and can be found if we persist in our search. Faith and belief that these positive methods can be discovered speeds us on to their manifestation. Faith turns our attention from a negative to a positive direction.

. . . Those Rose-Colored Glasses

Our imagery controls us. Remember poor Job from the Bible lessons. All that he feared came true. We are drawn to the experiences we subconsciously conceive and believe in. The best method to correct a bad habit of negative imagery is to anticipate it and voluntarily substitute positive images for negative ones.

Create a whole new collection of vivid inner pictures characterized by a sense of confidence and ease in yourself. These pictures will also embody a belief in yourself, in the good within everything, and in your ability to act courageously.

Whenever you find something bothering you, start some sort of positive affirmation. Hang on to it. Don't give worry a chance. Be adamant in your refusal to accept negative thoughts. Regardless of appearances, start affirming:

"I am healthy,"

"I am strong,"

"All is well,"

"I am loving,"

"I am powerful."

Or whatever other affirmation you need. Make your affirmation positive and say it in the present tense.

If there is a time lag between the "now" of your thoughts and the future manifestation of your affirmation, just keep repeating your positive statements. What is planted must take root. The harvest comes in due time. You have within you all the resources from the Source. Use them by affirming them.

When you repeat your affirmation, you impress your subconscious mind with just those qualities. Soon you will attract conditions that correspond perfectly in kind and quality. You remember that your subconscious mind does not argue or prove. Rather, it works to bring about conditions the conscious mind believes to be true. Think about and concentrate on what you want, NOT on what you don't want.

We are creatures of habit. When we change habits, we must be ever on guard. Remember that after the Israelites were freed, they had to cross the desert before the Promised Land was theirs. The desert represents the time period when everything seems to go against us. Whenever you change a course, you must be prepared to stop, go forward, go backward, stand still, and go forward again. Perhaps you will need to do this many times before the new habit is programmed. When we change the thinking habits of our subconscious mind, we must experience some associated difficulties.

Exterminating Factors

I've come up with a few suggestions to prevent old fears from holding us back.

1. **Light cancels darkness.** Don't lie in darkness and dwell on your fears. Get up and turn on the light.

   Many of the issues I've dealt with seemed overwhelming in the middle of the night. "I wish it were morning," I found myself saying. "Things will look better then."

2. **Face your fears.** Whatever you resist, persists.

   It's like an old king lion who's retired from active hunting responsibilities. He is assigned the job of roaring at approaching danger. Toothless and rather decrepit, he couldn't harm anyone. All he can do is roar. Most of our fears are like this old lion. When we face the fear, we find it has no teeth at all.

3. **Get the facts**. Feelings are not facts.

I remember the treat and mystery of staying overnight at my aunt's old farm house when I was a child. At night, my cousin and I mustered our courage and went upstairs together. Once in bed, we never moved. One night we heard scratching at the side of the house, right by the window in our room. No eyes closed that night.

The next morning, we were quite embarrassed to find that the scratching was made by an old tree branch brushing against the side of the house.

After you have the facts, then you can decide if the fear is justified.

4. **What your mind attends to is magnified**. Don't dwell on what you fear you cannot change.

A well-known prayer comes to mind:

God, grant me the serenity to accept the things I cannot change, courage to change the things I can and the wisdom to know the difference.

5. Don't buy into the fears of others.

I know a person who won't read the newspaper and barely watches TV. "I could scare myself to death," she tells me. Don't let others take liberties with your mind.

6. Limit the time you listen to others' fears.

As a therapist, I consciously limited the time patients spent talking about the negatives. Instead, I focused their attention on what to do now. Friendships sometimes are ended by a person's need to continually dwell on fears and worries.

Clogging Factor II - Holding a Grudge

Another "beta blocker" of your good is a grudge. Simply put, a grudge is the unresolved or unexpressed anger we feel towards someone whom we believe has wronged us. It's an emotional scab we pick at; eventually, it becomes infected, affects our relationships and possibly our health.

Persistent grudges lead to stress and physical problems. They can be very damaging to friends, family, and coworkers. We often use them as a form of punishment or as a protective mechanism against getting too close to others.

Excess Baggage

The carry-on baggage of a grudge-holder is packed with some pretty moldy traits:

1. Low self-esteem.
2. Intolerance.
3. Inability to look at events from the perspective of another.
4. Tendency to see oneself as a victim.
5. Lack of assertiveness.
6. Suspiciousness of others.
7. Hypersensitivity.

We can use our grudges as an excuse not to move ahead in life. "I've been dumped," you might say. "I'll just dwell on it to avoid any new relationship where I might be hurt again." A grudge can become the holder's favored crutch.

. . . Please Claim Your Grudge

An angry lover is afraid to express hostility directly. He or she fears it will cause a breakup. There is no reason in the world why a relationship should end because you express anger honestly and appropriately. You can never feel open and free with someone who holds a grudge.

Expressing anger is necessary for good health, both mental and physical. The manner in which it is expressed is a choice that leads to a successful, productive life or one of great pain, failure, and waste.

The greatest problem we face in dealing with our anger is determining how to discharge it in a socially acceptable manner and one that is healthy for us. To vent or not to vent, that is the question.

If we choose to vent anger, how do we go about doing so? Sometimes, we choose to just talk about it. However, we need to be cautioned that talking about an emotion doesn't necessarily reduce it; sometimes it just rehearses the pain and leaves us feeling angrier than before we first brought it up. It certainly is important to recognize the anger that we feel.

Once we recognize anger, most of us place the blame on a person or situation. It's natural to believe external events or people upset our balance. When we're angry with someone, it seems almost automatic that we make them the cause of all of our bad feelings. We say, "You made me mad," "You're getting on my nerves" or "You've ruined my life."

When we think like this, we only fool ourselves. No one else can make us angry. Yes, you heard me right! The bitter truth is that each of us creates every last ounce of anger and outrage we feel.

Recently, one of my grandsons angrily and with tearful outrage accused his mother, "You made me cry!" His mother responded so appropriately. "No, Jonathon," she said. "I told you what I felt. You chose to cry." This insight was spontaneous. Jonathon's mom was just as surprised as I was when she gave her son this response.

Before you become irritated or angry at any circumstance or person, you must first become aware of what is happening. You need to come to your own conclusions about the event. Your feelings are the result of how you interpret the event, not of the event itself.

Let's suppose angry thoughts have caused you to feel angry at someone. Perhaps your anger is an unconscious desire to make yourself feel guilty. But lashing out at someone else or holding in your anger is equally devastating to you and those around you.

It probably could be said, though, that consciously holding back anger is less damaging than unconsciously harboring angry feelings. Sometimes we know we're holding onto a grudge and we do so for many years.

It's not uncommon for long-standing relationships to end because of a person's unwillingness to give up and let go of an addiction to a hurt that happened years before. The hurt is called to mind and constantly replayed. It's as real today as it was when it was first interpreted. The intensity of resentment and anger equals the level experienced on the day the person first felt anger.

First of all, recognize the anger you're feeling. That may sound simple, but often it's the biggest obstacle faced by an angry person. We're often best at denying our anger, masking it, or labeling it something other than what it is. We feel guilty for feeling angry.

Next, decide what reward is gained by your continued anger. The reward might not be a positive one. It may even be a painful one that still rewards you in some fashion.

I have found that anger, as with any other emotion, has its rewards. What does it do for you to continue to feel angry? Some authorities suggest that an awareness of why you're angry will relieve some of the pressure.

When a reward is recognized and analyzed, the angry person can decide whether or not he or she wants to continue the response for whatever gratification is received from the reward. Perhaps the reward really isn't worth it after all. We sometimes need to ask ourselves if what we get out of our anger is worth all the energy we put into it.

Give the benefit of the doubt to the person or situation you're angry with. Given the knowledge we have available to us, most of what we do makes sense to us. It's been said that once you understand someone, it is impossible to hate him or her. Understanding another person doesn't mean that you agree, condone, or accept his behaviors. But this understanding makes it more difficult for you to respond in anger to him.

Once there is an understanding of the reasons and motivations of certain behaviors, it will be quite difficult to harbor a grudge or to nurse a resentment. Each of us has a reasonable explanation (at least to ourselves) for our behaviors.

I have also found that the very simple strategy of counting to ten does work! This helps us to gain control and cool down a bit. It's one of the easiest and most effective methods of reducing anger. There is really nothing to be gained from an explosive outburst aimed at retaliation. If you calm down first, then discussions frequently follow and they are much more rational ones.

There has been much written in the last few years about the importance of owning your anger. The initial tendency is to attack others. The first evidence of your attack on another is a statement which begins with "you": "You made me mad," "You hurt me." The truth of the matter is that I feel angry and I feel hurt. Any time an accusation begins with "you," it triggers a defensive response on the part of the other. It's an act of blaming another for your feelings.

Clogging Factor III - The Guilt

I once heard a minister say that thirty minutes is long enough for a person to feel guilty about anything. He went on to elaborate that nothing in the Bible urges us to wallow in remorse and guilt. We are not commanded to condemn and hate ourselves for our mistakes and blunders. Rather, we must recognize them, learn from them, and forgive ourselves.

In general, it seems that most people fall into two equally disastrous categories. Either they wallow in guilt and cannot forgive themselves, or they consider their actions and mistakes to be of no significance.

File it Under "G"

Unfortunately, time does not always diminish guilt. The memory may fade. The event may even be forgotten ... that is, stored away in the subconscious mind, repressed but very real.

Freud made a vital contribution with his discovery that memories are not forgotten or put into dead storage like an old trunk in the basement. A trunk full of ancient photographs, letters, and assorted junk does no damage in the basement. But every thought, emotion, and event has some effect on the personality.

No amount of rationalization diminishes guilt. The unconscious mind will not accept a rationalization, no matter how clever it is.

Real guilt can prick our conscience and keep us on the right track. You never truly forget doing something that created a deep sense of guilt.

I recall when I was eight or nine years old. I wasn't a real adventuresome child at that point in my life. I remember going one day to the grocery store and stealing a candy bar. I can see the grocery store just as clearly as if it were right in front of me now! I remember how I felt. I can see myself going out the back door and knowing that the whole world watched me do it. I can remember how bitter that candy tasted.

It took me a long time to get the courage to go back into that store because I felt that everyone knew I had stolen the candy bar. I truly experience that feeling over and over again whenever I think back on that incident. If I ever again thought about stealing anything, those memories and that awful feeling became checkpoints that kept me in line.

Interoffice Memo

The one enormous barrier which prevents us from accepting or loving ourselves properly is self-rejection. This is simply another term for self-hate. Suicide is the ultimate act of self-hate. This results from feelings of inferiority which were set in motion during childhood. We always tend to act in harmony with our self-image.

I've heard the stories:

People who have felt inadequate, inferior or guilty for as long as they can remember.

Parents who repeatedly told their children, "You're dumb," "You'll never amount to anything," "You're lazy," "You're like your no-good father." On and on they go.

These words are hammered in. The victims believe them implicitly. What alternative do children have but to believe their parents? They are the ultimate authorities in the lives of young children.

As adults, these children describe years of broken relationships and job losses. They talk of avoiding challenges and refusing to seek new opportunities. Still others go on to achieve great things and fight hard to overcome their self-rejection. But still they cannot completely eradicate the concept of their worthlessness, guilt, and inferiority.

Baseball pitcher Satchel Paige once uttered a profound truth: "Don't look back. Something may be gaining on you." There is wisdom in this because to always look back in remorse is self-defeating. However, these words reveal only a partial truth. There is value in looking back to discover how we became the people we are. We do this, not to blame ourselves, but to rid ourselves of undeserved blame.

. . . Who Dictated This Mess?

What we come to know is that there is no blame attached when we understand how our parents damaged us. They were also damaged by their parents. They simply passed on a heritage that has been passed down through the ages.

Oftentimes, all the love and approval we sought from our parents was not given because they didn't receive it themselves. As a result, they didn't even know what love and approval was. It's difficult to give something that you do not have.

Another thing we seem to hand down from one generation to the next is the manner in which feelings are expressed or not expressed. Perhaps you grew up in a home where feelings were openly expressed, shared, and demonstrated. You are blessed. I'm speaking of a home environment where you not only had permission to comfortably express feelings, but where you felt comfortable expressing what you truly felt without fear of judgment.

Such environments provide individuals with a real comfort in emotional expression. They can hug, touch and tell people how they feel with greater ease than those who have not grown up in such an environment.

It's been interesting for me to observe couples and find that these "huggers," who typically come from demonstrative households, always seem to attract and attach themselves to persons from non-hugging backgrounds. In marriage, these people complement each other in the area of emotional expression. But it also is a source of conflict. The person who can't feel and express as easily has a new challenge to develop a comfort zone of emotional expression.

... A Case in Point

Scott was referred to me for counseling by his family doctor. Scott was thirty-four years old, an engineer, a divorced man and the father of three little girls. The doctor said he had been seeing Scott for severe anxiety attacks and headaches. But he just couldn't put his finger on a physical problem. He suspected there was something else generating these physical reactions.

Scott came to see me. He was everything the doctor said he was: bright and intelligent. After he sat down, I asked him what it was like growing up in his home.

He told me there were four boys in his family. All were very athletic. They were tough. Each of them excelled in sports. After he spoke about his family environment for a while, I asked him what it was like emotionally growing up in his home. Were feelings shared? Did he ever see his parents show affection to each other?

Scott said it would only take a few seconds to describe his emotional background. "We just didn't deal with emotions at all. We were taught to be tough, not to cry. If we were hurt, we just put it inside and kept going. Being vulnerable was not a part of that image of toughness."

As he went on, I asked him about his ex-wife's family.

"They're great huggers," he said, "I walk in the house and everybody puts their arms around me and everybody's kissing everybody."

Then I asked him if one of the reasons for his divorce was that his wife felt unloved by him. He said that for more than thirteen years, during the period of his marriage, his wife felt emotionally starved in her relationship with him. Being such a good, logical thinker, Scott probably had sound answers for all their conflicts. But emotionally, he was a void.

"Oh, yes," Scott explained, "many times my wife said that some way, some how, she wanted emotional feedback from me. I really didn't have much tolerance for this need of hers." Scott went on to say that after thirteen years, his wife felt that the lack of nurturing in their relationship was intolerable.

As the session ended, Scott asked if he could come back and talk more about this. I challenged him in a different way. "I don't believe you need to talk more about it. I think you need to do something that will help you discover your emotions, this unknown dimension of yourself that has previously been on hold." I suggested that he approach some of his friends and share this dimension with them.

It would be a new experience. It would initially be somewhat awkward. He would experience some fear for his own vulnerability. After he had risked several times in different situations, I then wanted him to return to continue our sessions.

Approximately one month later, the phone rang. It was

Scott. I hardly recognized his voice. It was full of emotion. (This frequently happens when someone opens up and unleashes a great emotional backlog that had been stock-piled for years.) When he came in later, he told me what he had done.

"I left your office that day," he said. "I took your challenge and went to a pay phone to call my ex-wife." (He was at a ten on his pain thermometer!) "I asked if I could come over and see her. It was overwhelming to both of us as I shared with her what I was beginning to discover. I admitted that she had every right to expect emotional nurturing in a relationship. I wanted to accept my share of the responsibility for our failed marriage."

Before he left, Scott told me he and his former wife were sobbing in each others' arms. His wife asked him, "Is this the same Scott I was married to?"

As the weeks went on, Scott became increasingly angry with his parents. Although he admitted it might be unfair, he wondered why three of the boys were now divorced. Did they struggle with this same fear of vulnerability? Did they also not know how to share or to nurture others?

Scott went over to see his parents. In his conversation with them, a lot of his anger, frustration, and pent up feelings came out. When he finished, he was not prepared for what his father said in response.

"I never thought that I would admit this to you," his father began, "but I was a little jealous of you when you were a little boy. My father, your grandfather, had a way of holding you on his lap, putting his arms around you and pulling you close to him. I can hear him now telling you how much he loved you. I used to watch that and think that

I didn't remember having that happen to me. I guess I didn't do that to you because it wasn't done to me. I didn't think about how important and necessary it was."

I often reflect on this example and testimonial. Too many times each of us is caught in the same "hand-me down" behavior trap. It's important for us to remember, all things considered, that our parents did as well as they knew how to do with the knowledge they had and so are you.

Freeing Factor II - Forgiveness

Most of us carry big, deep, and undeserved hurts: the disloyalty of a friend, the abuse of a parent, the betrayal of a lover. It may have happened yesterday, last year, five years ago, or even a lifetime ago. It was personal and unfair.

I remember a couple who ended a thirty-five year marriage. The wife could not or chose not to tolerate the blame and pain she felt when her husband repeatedly and vindictively lashed out at her. The husband blamed her for something her mother said to him nearly twenty years before. She felt caught by something she truly had no control over. But her husband still used the incident as a vehicle for his anger.

He chose not to forgive her mother for the affront. According to him, he was more than justified in carrying this anger with him. He expected his wife to pick up the tab and accept the guilt. The marriage ended because of his unwillingness to forgive a mother-in-law for words spoken years before.

More Than a Band-Aid

I'm sure this sort of situation has occurred regularly in many of our lives. In looking back at these times, we might have said, "I'm sorry," or "Please forgive me," or "I forgive you." We didn't choose to do this, however. The only real culprits in these situations are our egos; the only real losers are ourselves.

Many of these hurts, done to us by others, are personal and unfair. They go so deep that they cannot be forgotten. For many, these memories, fueled by anger and hate, cloud the present and shackle the future like an insidious cancer of the spirit. There is a cure, a healing balm called forgiveness. Although a most difficult and often misunderstood concept, it still is the only remedy for the flow of pain that looms from out of the past.

Forgiving is not a matter of being nice to someone who has been rotten to you. It's not an obligation. Do you remember when you were young and your parents told you to forgive someone? It felt like a true obligation, because we certainly didn't feel like doing so. It is not a moral obligation to be nice, but it is a moral right not to go on being hurt by hurts that weren't fair in the first place.

Forgiveness gives you permission to stop hurting. When you've had it up to ten on your pain thermometer and are willing to give up that pain and be healed, then is the time for forgiveness. We must realize, however, that by constantly dwelling on old wounds, we bind them more tightly to us. We must be willing to give up this devastating addiction and attachment to pain.

In Remission

Forgiving is not agreeing with, condoning, or excusing another's hurtful acts. It isn't a mushy desire to absolve everybody of blame. It is not toleration of another's abuse.

The healing process of forgiveness does not require reconciliation. It does not necessarily involve a friendship reborn or a love relationship rebuilt. Sometimes you can start over and sometimes you can't. The other person, you know, may choose not to accept your forgiveness or give his own in return. Perhaps the other person has died and you can't turn back the clock.

What you have control over is whether or not you're going to wallow in the misery of your hurt and hate or whether you're going to heal yourself. Don't wait for another to give in. It could be a long wait. Don't wait for an opportunity to "get even," because you never will. Be patient with yourself. Forgiving, for most of us, comes along slowly in small steps. It builds upon itself and it takes time. Forgiving is a process and, while you're involved in it, forgetting becomes easier.

One way to check on whether you're healing is to recall the incident and note whether it is remembered without anger or hurt. Sadness may well be an emotional response to the memory, but not the original feelings we had when we held the grudge. The emotional responses are changing.

Off to the Clinic

I had a very personal experience with forgiveness. There

was a time in my life when I needed inner healing. This occurred when I was taking one of those tougher courses in life and found myself stuck.

I enrolled in a three-day workshop called "Inner Healing." I thought, perhaps, I would learn something that would be of use to me and that I could possibly share with others.

... Day 1

The first day of the workshop was devoted to forgiving others and to letting go of all our unmet expectations and disappointments. I didn't have any trouble with this first day. It's never been difficult for me to forgive and even to forget what others have done in the past. This was, however, very difficult for many of the course participants, because of the deep pain they had experienced. However, everyone attempted to begin the process, and that's really what it's all about when you forgive.

... Day 2

The second day was spent forgiving God. Again, this was somewhat of a surprise to me, because I don't blame God for situations in my life. I do feel that I have a responsibility for whatever happens to me. To blame God for the circumstances and consequences of my life is to fail to accept responsibility for the same events. For many, this forgiveness of God was difficult, because events and tragedies sometimes happen to us and we just can't immediately see our connection to them.

I had a secretary who had this very trouble. She chose to never forgive God for the death of a family member many years prior to our relationship. She truly felt that God was not only the cause, but certainly could have prevented the tragedy.

I don't have any ready answers for such tragedies. But through the years, I listened to her anger as it filtered through in her biting, cutting sense of humor. It was most often demonstrated, however, by her outright anger at God. She refused to discuss God in any way. She felt that it was indeed appropriate to blame God.

But sometimes anger towards God comes through when we ask, "Why me?" When we ask this question, we're probably looking for an outside force to blame for the events we're experiencing. Again, this dimension of forgiveness was not difficult for me to deal with.

. . . Day 3

The final day was difficult for me. It was then that I realized the real challenge of the healing process and learned what forgiving was really about. It was learning to forgive myself. It took courage to face the truth that I really had hurt others and had done things that were contemptible and demeaning. It's always a risk to accept guilt, but there's no self-forgiveness unless there's truth first.

Forgiving ourselves for being less than we thought we should be or could be can be a trap. We end up being very critical and judgmental of ourselves. Our real challenge is to forgive our whole selves and not to dissect them to the point where we reinforce our sense of unworthiness. Learning to appreciate that we did what we did with the knowledge we had at the time is to learn to appreciate our own human vulnerability.

A Lasting Cure

The big decision we must make is whether we want to be rid of the pain. The more we're stuck in our pain, the more likely it is that we must decide what to do with it. It is possible that we want to keep our hateful feelings and we also want peace of mind. We can't have both, however. We must develop a sense of compassion towards ourselves.

I have had clients who I felt certain could not be helped by counseling. They had already tried, condemned, sentenced and hung themselves by a jury of one. They could not admit they were not a finished product in the course work of their earthly classes. Nor could they accept that there would be mistakes made and new learning to be accomplished.

At the end of the three-day workshop, I was well aware that to forgive is truly to achieve inner healing. Simple, but not easy. When it's accomplished, we have probably come the closest to touching Love in its purest form.

The management of our feelings will probably be the greatest challenge we face as we attempt to manage our lives. If we believe that feelings are facts that cannot change, then we will be victims. The most painful times I've experienced in my journey have been those times when I thought my feelings were out of control. It was as though the decision-maker, the choice-maker in me was rendered helpless.

As I regained control, I realized that the choice was mine to make. Only then did the pain lessen and my life become more balanced. I learned that I could choose how I interpreted the circumstances of my life. Each different interpretation generated a different emotional response from me. It was one of the greatest, most miraculous turning points of my life.

Love is What it's All About

Every human being born into this world is created with the innate capacity to give and receive Love. If I'm angry at someone, I realize that anger is just my desire to feel guilty. I know that Love and guilt cannot coexist. I have to choose between the two and I choose Love. Love is what it's all about.

Think of the whole spectrum of Love: caring, concern, positive regard, compassion, friendship, affection, romantic love, agape love, and benevolence. It becomes apparent that this is one of the strongest human drives.

Read My Lips

Love is most often expressed in actions. We recognize these actions, one of which is listening. Listening is truly an act of Love. Who listens to children? Parents instruct them, lecture them, order them around, and scold them. But seldom does one find a parent who takes the time to listen. On the rare occasions when a parent might listen and detect something that needs to be corrected in the child's thinking, that's the signal to start up another lecture.

One of the most common complaints in my counseling sessions was: "My husband won't talk. He's uncommunicative. I'm dying for someone to talk to." Spouses who do not communicate fall into one of two categories. They are either innately incapable of carrying on an intelligent conversation or they have been turned off by criticism, argument, or an overtalkative mate.

One husband reported that his wife complained of his being withdrawn and uncommunicative. "I don't talk very much at home," this man said. "I'm much more spontaneous and talkative at work. I don't get shot down and criticized there." He talked at length about the conflicts at home. "I often appear disinterested at home, but I can't help it. At the office, we have more fun in a week than we do at home in six months. We don't tear each other apart at work. We accept each other and I don't feel accepted at home."

These are not at all uncommon comments and complaints from family members. The people who live the closest to us often are the very ones we don't listen to very effectively. Perhaps one of the reasons for this is because it's hard work.

As a therapist, it takes energy to completely attend to another person. It's also a risky situation, because when we truly listen to another person, we risk having to change our own minds. Once we understand this person, it is difficult to judge or resent him or her.

The Source of Love

The Love we're discussing here is not of a romantic sort or even an affectionate love. It's the Love given to us by the Source. Love is a spiritual gift. And it may surprise you to know that it is not an emotion. It is often mistaken for an emotion, because it is expressed as a feeling, just as emotions are.

Love, though, is a spiritual quality. It is drawn on to settle emotion and to balance our feelings. More often than not, Love is surrounded by emotion to such a degree that we confuse it with emotion. Therefore, it is commonly thought that Love includes turbulence and stress. This is not true.

Emotion can include turbulence and stress. It can even accompany Love. But emotion is not actually the divine gift of Love.

No Strings Attached

Love is energy. Energy that uplifts and purifies the emotions. You may ask, "How can I tell if I'm experiencing genuine Love for another or if it's emotion?" There is one way you can always tell. Ask yourself whether or not there are any conditions attached to your Love for this person. Must they act a certain way in order for you to love them? Must they love you in return in order to receive your Love? Do you require that they have certain beliefs?

In other words, if you place conditions on your Love toward another, then it is not Love. It is emotionalism which results in what we call conditional love. Most of us recognize conditional love from our human experiences. We were loved if we achieved. We were loved if we pleased. We were loved if we were good, and on and on.

The Love, however, that is the Source is unconditional Love. When Jesus called upon us to love our enemies, he was not suggesting approval or affection. Rather, he asked that we show an unconditional, positive regard and concern to our enemies in spite of any personal feelings we might have for them. This enemy may well be a relative, a parent, a husband, wife, brother or sister. The enemy may be you, or that part of yourself that you find unacceptable.

We are not commanded to love the evil within ourselves or others. But we are instructed to love the total person as God does. Unconditional Love transcends external differences and joins us all together with a sense of "oneness."

Best Wishes

Love is your ability to desire that only good come to all. We live in a world consciousness of limitation. It's easy to believe that there is only so much good to go around.

If you believe that there is only so much Love, then you are likely to experience jealousy. There is only so much food, or so much money. When you believe this, then you begin to think that you had better get what's yours before someone else takes it.

Love is unlimited, because the Source, which is Love, is

infinite. It seeks only good for all. Love is also a promise. It's a promise that our innermost desires will come true. Love has the power to bring any of our noble dreams into physical reality. Any hope or desire which is right for us, if visualized and surrounded by Love and given thanks for, will come true.

Love is magnetic. It draws all things to it. If you love a person or object, you draw it to you. You can even draw negative conditions, because you subconsciously love them. It is amazing how little we consciously use the magnetizing power of Love. It is most often utilized unconsciously.

Love is the great harmonizer. When Love draws things together, it is always done in a peaceful manner. Chaotic situations are dissolved when Love is present.

Love is a healer. Love can heal the body, the mind, the emotions and the spirit within.

Send My Love

Our task is to emit Love, sending it out to those around us. We don't have to force it. It automatically does the right thing.

When we look at others through the eyes of Love, there is no condemning or judging. It allows a person to grow and to find his or her rightful place on this earth. Love brings freedom.

When you Love others, you free them to be the persons they were meant to be. When people are free, they are then open to the harmony and peace that resides in and around them.

Henry Drummond, author of **The Greatest Thing in The World**[1], had this in mind when he said:

"Life is full of opportunities for learning love. The world is not a playground, it is a school room. Life is not a holiday, but an education and the one eternal lesson for all of us, how better we can love."

When we contemplate Love at its highest possible level, it's difficult to grasp with our finite minds. When we ponder the experiences of Love in our own lives, we recall such things as the first smiles we received from our children, the way we felt on our wedding days, and the thrills of loving relationships with a special person. We try to recapture how it felt. The feelings we recall are but small evidence of the Love waiting for us from the true Source.

We have been given the responsibility of allowing this Love to flow through us. What we often do is fail to manage our feelings appropriately. Consequently, we stop Love's flow. Nothing stops it sooner than our fears, our guilts, and our unresolved anger.

Our feelings are our choices. The challenge we have is to change our own thoughts, a change that allows for different responses which open us up to the experience of this great gift. It is waiting for us. We must tap the well and assume our responsibility in the search for this gift of Love.

(1) Henry Drummond, **The Greatest Thing in The World** (London: Collins, Ltd., 1953.)

176

Chapter Five

Stay Alive
as Long as You Live

Much of your pain is self-chosen. It is the bitter potion
by which the physician within you heals your sick self.

Kahlil Gibran

Obviously the question of good health has no simple answer. There are thousands of factors that affect our attitudes and vulnerability to illness, not the least of which, we would like to think, are heredity and the hand of Fate.

Many researchers who study this phenomenon are convinced that the deciding factor is firmly within our control. Happiness or misery, health or illness: these are choices each of us make. This is not an easy concept to accept. If you're having trouble swallowing it, don't be alarmed!

How you got to where you are is not as important as taking control of your situation **now**. It's necessary to understand how we unconsciously and even consciously undermine our own well-being.

Striking a Balance

Some experts believe that ninety percent of our stress and illnesses comes from the beliefs, expectations, thoughts and feelings we have about ourselves. Seen from this perspective, illness and stress serve as messages from our bodies. They direct us to explore basic questions about feelings, needs, values, and life goals.

The symptoms of an illness signal not an inability to manage the outside world, but a disconnection inside ourselves. This disconnection requires that we search for improved inner self-management. When illness does occur, it is an opportunity to examine ourselves and our circumstances. Illness may indicate that we've gotten out of balance and that we need to be more compassionate with ourselves. When disease develops, it may give us a clue to make adjustments within ourselves or in our response to the world around us.

Good health means having the flexibility and the inner resources to respond to both assaults and opportunities. It is more than the absence of illness or disease. We will always be exposed to germs and viruses, emotional shocks, and potential physical injuries. But when we are healthy, our bodies and minds are able to rise and meet life's challenges. Good health means that we participate in the dynamic web of life.

Getting There

Health is not a static state of perfection. It is the process of interacting with everything around and inside of us in ways that promote growth and vitality. In this context, "healing" is the process of starting wherever we are now and making incremental changes in our attitudes and actions to encourage health. Oriental medicine has known for a millennium that mind and body are one. Both can be viewed as a continuum, with mental well-being carrying over to the physical or the other way around.

People respond to the modern world with a body and a mind. The maintenance of health requires self-awareness and balance. At any given time in our lives, there are many forces influencing our health. Among these factors are nutrition, exercise, stress, genetic predisposition, psychosocial factors, and purely medical factors such as injury or infection. The question is whether some of these factors become disproportionate influences that result in illness, or whether the factors maintain an optimal balance that promotes good health.

Today's growing health consciousness places great emphasis on the body. The result has been very positive. People are exercising and eating healthier foods. But by concentrating our energy on the physical aspects of good health alone, we neglect a more important dimension of health. We tend to equate the body with the person and this is a mistake. We are as much a sum total of our thoughts, feelings, and insights as we are of our flesh and bones. When we focus on the body, we think of health as an end in itself. We spend all our time eating the right foods, taking the appropriate vitamins, doing the right exercises. We become obsessed with our bodies and narrow our focus to physical goals.

A Paradox

Perhaps a more important question that is frequently overlooked is, "How can we use a healthy body to accomplish our life goals?" The body is a vehicle that transports us to our destination. Health is a means and not an end. A healthy body is something we utilize to live in a meaningful and rich way.

Some individuals are healthy in body. Some are not. It's as important to be healthy in mind as in body. We need to ask ourselves if we are using our physical capacity to accomplish our purpose in life. There are people who are healthy physically but who do not live a healthy life. For such individuals, life has no value, direction, or purpose.

There are also people who are quite ill who lead very rich lives. I consider these individuals to be much healthier than those who simply have physical health and no reason to live. The will to live is an undeniably powerful force in our health and survival. It may very well be the most powerful force influencing health and healing. There are a great many people who are sick and have lost their life's purpose. But there are many others who are sick and have found greater meaning in life as a result of their illnesses.

Sometimes, illness results in positive outcomes. We can learn an invaluable lesson by studying the way Eastern cultures view illness. To these cultures, an illness is not necessarily a disaster or crisis. Rather, it is an experience that can represent the beginning of a whole new way of looking at life.

It's All in Your Mind

If we are to seriously seek better health, we must come to grips with some startling and challenging ideas about health. The first is that the causes of poor health are not so much outside ourselves as they are within our attitudes and beliefs. What we feel and think have a definite influence on our bodies.

For example, when a person becomes angry, a detrimental chemical action takes place in the body. Acids are secreted into the system. If this persists over a period of time, these acids will eventually erode some part of the body. The effects of this action are seen in the development of stomach ulcers.

Every action of thought, positive or negative, initiates a chemical reaction in the body. Negative emotions can affect the heart rate and blood pressure. The mental/emotional influence on the body is referred to as a psychosomatic illness. It is now believed that as much as eighty percent of all physical conditions of poor health are psychosomatic. Negative responses are learned. Therefore, we can also unlearn, retrain, or recondition ourselves with positive and constructive responses that pay rich dividends in the form of improved health.

What's Your AQ?

Medical and psychological researchers agree that self-esteem and a positive outlook are potent factors in the ability of our bodies to resist disease. Stresses such as family conflicts, job dissatisfaction, loss of a loved one, personal failures, overwork, and major life changes lessen our immune responsiveness.

Our mental reactions to these stressors determine our susceptibility to disease. In other words, some people become ill after psychological stress more frequently than after physical stress or exposure to disease entities.

We might feel low in confidence and helpless to influence the course of our lives. We might feel we lack the means of self-expression, that we have no positive vision for the future. We might feel isolated from love and support. In these times, we are most likely to succumb to illness.

On the other hand, high self-esteem, good coping skills, self-expression, an ability to find satisfaction and support, self-awareness, and a feeling that there is a place for us in the world all increase our resistance to disease. You feel the way you think.

Let's take a little quiz to measure your "Attitude Quotient" (or AQ).

1. You create a brilliant work of art for which you are highly commended. Do you feel:

   a. Proud and deserving of the praise, confident that continued efforts will lead to continued public acclaim? Or

   b. Awkward and unworthy of such acclaim, certain that this success was just "dumb luck" and that you'll never be able to achieve such acclaim again?

2. You are just about to make a right turn into the next lane when you glance out of the corner of your eye and notice another car suddenly within inches of you. Do you feel:

   a. Relieved and grateful that the car missed you? Or

   b. Shaken and distraught by the near brush with disaster?

3. Several members of your family have experienced high blood pressure. Do you feel:

   a. That you have a choice in managing your life, your body, and your health in a way that will avert this condition? Or

   b. That you are destined to experience the sam e physical problem?

Whether you chose the positive "a" answers or the more negative "b" answers, these three examples illustrate a point. Situations don't change your moods. You feel the way you think. How you think, then, has a profound effect on your physical and emotional health.

People who constantly see themselves and life in a negative light create for themselves a state of low self-esteem and depression. They also burden their bodies with unrelenting stress. Every time you think the worst, your body reacts as if it were actually experiencing that tension-filled situation. Your "fight or flight" instincts are called to action. Adrenaline flows, your pulse quickens and you dwell on these thoughts. Exhaustion soon results. Where the mind goes, your energy flows.

Not surprisingly, negative thinkers frequently suffer from stress-related physical ailments. Contrary to popular belief, negative or positive thinkers aren't born with these habits of thought.

These thinking patterns arise from our experiences. Psychologists tell us that the way we perceive any situation is, to a large extent, an automatic thought response. "Automatic," in this sense, is similar to the natural way we tie our shoes, or the smoker's spontaneous reach for a cigarette.

It's a learned response. It's filed in the computer of your mind, ready for instant recall and activation. It's a kind of habit we develop over time by absorbing the attitudes or those around us (parents, teachers, peers, and media idols). You don't even know it's happening because it is subconscious.

Day after day, week after week, messages are put into your subconscious mind. Something happens and you automatically "know" what it means. A friend doesn't return your call and you just "know" you did something to offend him or her. Something was done behind your back and he or she is embarrassed to talk to you. More realistic, however, is the possibility that your friend is just bogged down at work.

This kind of automatic thinking goes on constantly during the course of a day. Silently in your head, you carry on a conversation with yourself, interpreting situations, making judgments about people.

Depending on the nature of your experiences, this self-talk can be a barrage of self-doubt and self-criticism:

"I'll never be able to finish this project on time."

"I know I'll say the wrong thing."

"No one can be trusted."

"I don't deserve it."

It's possible, however, to direct this self-talk in a more positive direction. In other words, the voice inside of you can say, "Things will work out," "I can handle it," "He likes me," or "I do deserve it."

AQ = HQ

Oftentimes, these vague, unfocused, negative thoughts lurking just below the surface of our consciousness do more harm than those dragged out into the open. In other words, our AQ can greatly impact our HQ, our "Health Quotient."

The first step to get out of this rut is to become aware of what you're actually thinking and feeling. Sometimes this is more difficult than it sounds, because these thoughts tend to be well disguised.

Perhaps we need to implement a technique utilized in the sports world: the instant replay. Think back to what crossed your mind just prior to a mood change or a physical sensation (for instance, fatigue, heaviness, or butterflies in the stomach.) Sometimes it appears there is no preceding thought. But later, you can attribute a certain mood to a specific feeling.

Another way to become aware of negative thoughts is to count them. Try to keep track over a period of time — even for just an hour — of how many times you respond negatively in a verbal or mental manner. You will probably be shocked to realize the amount of energy you expend in a negative direction.

We must all tune into our self-talk, because we often have difficulty being objective and looking at an issue without emotion. For example, as I mentioned previously, you might be waiting for a return phone call. As you wait, you conjure up all sorts of self-defeating reasons for why the call has not come. The reality simply is that you are waiting for a phone call.

Shifting Gears

The secret is to stop our negative thoughts and change our interpretations. This change results in a different feeling response. Look at the facts as they **are**, not as you **think** they are.

Once you're able to identify and clarify thought patterns that make you feel badly, you will then be able to answer them. You must substitute another interpretation of the event in order to achieve a different feeling. In other words, your phone call will be returned at the convenience of a very busy individual.

In addition to answering your negative thoughts, you must want to act on the new thoughts and beliefs. If your call is not returned, you will either call again or wait until you see the individual in person. The bottom line is that a negative perception of yourself is the real culprit.

I'm All Ears

At the beginning of some of my seminars, I ask the question, "How many of you talk to yourselves?" A chuckle runs through the audience and about seventy-five percent raise their hands. Then I ask, "How many of you get answers?" Another chuckle and twenty-five percent raise their hands. A third question is next asked. "How many of you ever interrupt yourselves?" One hand goes up.

To me, this indicates a lack of awareness on the part of many of us. We lack an awareness of our thinking patterns as well as an awareness of the impact that our thoughts have on our lives. The thoughts that many individuals have about themselves are negative ones. These people tend to accept negative thoughts without challenging them and they act as though the thoughts were true.

Take Affirmative Action

The old critic in our heads can really dominate our thoughts. For every critic there can be an automatic "answer" of guilt, rejection, rebellion, depression, and helplessness. In short, an answer to all the self-defeating emotional responses that have ever been programmed into our automatic subconscious computer.

We need to interrupt the chain by limiting the domination of the critic. When it speaks, we challenge its authority. "What evidence do you have for this accusation?" we ask. "You have failed to see my strengths and focus only on my weaknesses. How do you know I can't do that?" we add. "Who are you to say that I'm unworthy?" This self-talk is the first step in our becoming aware of just who is in charge. We are! We can choose a kinder, more loving and nurturing manner of speaking to ourselves.

Affirmations are positive, personal statements that modify negative beliefs and values. Affirmations change the direction of our mind's focus, a change of attention.

At the core of such popular books as Dale Carnegie's **How To Win Friends and Influence People,** and Norman Vincent Peale's **The Power of Positive Thinking** is the belief that people should consciously attempt to modify their inner conversations and assumptions. An almost immediate improvement in performance is accomplished by this means. Energy levels increase. Remember, where your mind goes, your energy flows; whatever gets your attention becomes magnified.

Positive Relationships

It is most important that we check our own positive thinking patterns, because the people in our lives are mirror reflections of ourselves. If we choose to think negatively, we'll likely find other negative thinkers surrounding us.

Positive people have positive relationships. Love and health go hand in hand. The mandate to, "Love your neighbor as yourself" is not just a moral mandate. It's a physiological one. Something deep inside of us responds positively to others when we love ourselves. Love has a way of sparking healthy biological reactions in much the same way as good food and fitness. When people have close relationships they feel less threatened, less alone, more confident, and more in control. The knowledge that we have people we can turn to in times of need provides us with very important feelings of security, optimism, and hope. All of these positive feelings serve as great antidotes to illness and stress.

Beware the Virus

We are often warned to avoid negative people. I'm sure that many of us have had an experience similar to the following. We get up in the morning and look forward to the day with positive expectations. But then we go to work and sit next to a person who views life in a very negative manner. It requires effort on our part to maintain a positive outlook. The danger is that little by little the negativism of our co-worker seeps into our minds. We begin to find evidence to support a negative outlook. We join our co-workers in their dismal anticipation of all that life has to offer. By mid-morning, it's likely we find ourselves in a group, all of us complaining about something we never considered previously.

As an outsider traveling around the country, in and out of schools and businesses, it's always interesting for me to visit the break room. It's often a breeding ground for negativism. I find people, often in groups, complaining about things and commiserating with each other about supposed unfairness and tragedy.

One of the best measurements of a company's or a school's success is the quality of its discontent. Interactions with others impact us all in very real ways. Each of us has a powerful influence on others. We are contagious, in either a positive or a negative manner.

Contagious People

The power of one personality to influence many is quite real. My friend lives in an apartment building which has been under the management of three different individuals. The first managers were a couple who loved people because they loved themselves. Their influence on all the tenants was one of love, acceptance, and fellowship.

They were like magnets. They attracted all the tenants to them and to their wonderful outlook. They were very comfortable and free to be themselves without fear or criticism. There were many get-togethers, holiday parties, and impromptu gatherings when someone hosted a pot-luck or a poolside barbecue. The personalities of the managers were so positive and accepting that people reflected these qualities in their interactions with neighbors.

There was a change of managers, however. The new manager did not like people. She was bitter, negative, moody, and very critical. It wasn't long before people ceased to congregate at the mail room. No longer did they feel comfortable sitting and chatting with one another. The holiday festivities stopped and the impromptu gatherings did too. The residents remained in their apartments, avoiding any confrontations with this manager.

One person's personality changed the entire atmosphere in a building from one of warmth, joy, acceptance, and caring, to one of coldness, fear, indifference, and intimidation.

Never underestimate the power of your attitude on others. It certainly challenges us to remember that we have a choice in **how** we think. It's most important to not allow the negative attitudes of a group or individual to influence your attitudes.

Preventive Medicine

Sometimes we find ourselves confronted with a negative personality situation. It's possible to think of it impersonally, although we generally interpret everything that happens in our lives in a personal manner. We might find ourselves saying: "They don't pay me enough because they don't appreciate me." "They don't think I'm good enough. That's why I didn't get a raise." "They don't want to come over because they don't like my cooking." These all might be common declarations of personal interpretations.

These personal interpretations build up tension and frustration. We should always remind ourselves that our happiness is not dependant on what others do or on their opinions of us. We should not limit our good in life simply because someone has a negative interpretation of us or what we're doing. It's most often an interpretation made without real facts.

We certainly should not feel we can't be happy simply because another rejects us. Our true worth is not determined by position, power or money any more than our potential is determined by an IQ test.

All personal assessments are limited. They are based on subjective opinions rather than objective facts. The same thing applies to what I think of myself on a personal level.

We often give others a "blank check" which allows them to draw whatever they want out of us. The person you're angry with draws out of your personal fund, because you gave him or her the power to do so. This person is in control.

Why should we accept someone's assessment of us, since most personal assessments are limited in the first place? We can control what we think about ourselves. But we cannot control what others think about us. We can only refuse to accept their opinions and views.

No doubt, you've heard the following statement (or said it many times yourself): "He makes me sick!" It's not the person himself who makes you sick. It's the negative thoughts about that person. When we learn to control our thoughts and feelings, then we can describe ourselves as "mature."

Be Your Own Best Friend

Loneliness may be hazardous to your health in a concrete way. If people feel lonely, it has nothing to do with the number of people around them. Rather, their loneliness results from their expectations of life and their reactions to their environments. These are risk factors you can do something about.

Research does not support the view that loneliness is a consequence of living alone. Loneliness is often a synonym for boredom. People who spend their time alone in creative endeavors learn to deal with solitude. In this process, they begin to feel more calm, creative, and happy. You must be secure within yourself before you can find contentment in solitude.

The problem is that we often grow up in the constant company of others. We come to depend on others for our happiness. When experiences such as death or divorce force us into "solitary confinement," then our self-confidence is put to the test.

I grew up on a farm, without television, and with lots of hours to be alone. I'm grateful for this experience. I learned early in life to be creative and self-sufficient when I had many hours of free time and solitude. I have worked with many clients who grew up in quite different conditions. They were raised in large families and might have had roommates at school. Perhaps they even married immediately after graduation from high school. They found it very painful when they found themselves divorced or alone for some reason. The adjustment was virtually impossible. When you find yourself alone, view it as an opportunity to discover yourself.

The first indication that we are in trouble with our own mental health is when we are preoccupied with ourselves. Individuals who dwell too much on themselves — even if they don't consider themselves to be lonely or bored — are probably not enjoying enough good contact with others. Having healthful, enriching experiences with others is the best protection against loneliness.

No Harm Done

It seems obvious that we would never wish to harm our own bodies. And yet it's done everyday by individuals not unlike ourselves. A balanced diet is one of the basics. If you don't eat properly, your body is not nourished. The brain suffers as well. We are becoming a nation of health-conscious individuals. However, when you consider the growing number of weight loss centers and published diets, it becomes apparent that although we **know** what's good for us, we **choose** to do otherwise. Many have the perception that they are invulnerable and indestructible.

A recent television interview program featured smokers as guests. These people had experienced repeated heart and respiratory ailments. They continued to smoke in spite of their knowledge of the dangers of cigarettes and the repeated pleading and nagging from loved ones. The same compulsive behaviors are seen in alcoholics and drug abusers (and even in people with certain food obsessions where the physical body is at risk or under stress).

Once again, the bottom line for such destructive patterns is self-esteem. If we acknowledge our self-worth and alter our self-talk, we can make major changes in our bodies and in our lives. It is easier when you banish negative thought patterns from your mind first and then replace them with positive ones.

If you truly love another, you would not wish him or her physical harm. The same goes for truly loving yourself. You would not do anything that would create physical harm. Addictions which cause harm represent an imbalance within our minds and bodies. They are the result of losing touch with ourselves, of always reaching outside for stimulation and satisfaction, because we no longer find gratification within.

Another factor further complicates this challenge of finding happiness within ourselves. We live in a society that stresses outside stimulation. The theory that we have the **right** to instant gratification is fed to us repeatedly through the media. This concept forces us to look outside ourselves for what can only be found within. The quickest way to get someone on the path to self-discovery is to introduce him to the concept that each of us has a "wise self" within.

Stretch, Reach and Limber Up

Our organisms are not made for monotony. Our bodies need change in order to thrive. But we humans are often obsessed with predictability. The two things that drive us to a state of predictability are our need for security and our need for comfort. Once we satisfy our definition of security, we then give ourselves permission to step outside the comfort zones and do something different with our lives. This process is called taking a risk.

To not risk in your life is the surest way of losing your life. Eventually your life is destroyed. You never learn who you are. You never test your potential and never stretch or reach. You become comfortable with fewer and fewer experiences. Your world shrinks and you become rigid. In other words, you become a victim of your environment. Not to risk is to rust or even to rot.

There is no way to grow without taking chances. Sure, it's scary. Sure, it's uncertain. But in order to step forward, you have to leave a known and secure place behind. This is another illustration of getting to ten on your pain thermometer. You're willing to risk because not risking costs you more. In every risk there is an unavoidable loss. We can't move on to the next level without leaving something behind that was familiar and comfortable. If this doesn't frighten you a little, then the risk is probably not worthy of you. No risk worth taking can ever be completely secure. There is always an unknown factor or it would not be considered a risk.

My life has been full of such risks. I have willingly started my life over four times. Each time, I left behind what

I considered to be my security. Those risks were calculated risks. That doesn't mean that I had financial or people resources around me that would ensure my success. But it did mean that my potential gain appeared greater than any potential loss. I felt I stood a reasonable chance of coming out on the plus side. It was worth the effort.

Pace Yourself

There are those who risk for the sake of risking. I'm not that kind of risk-taker. I have always known that within all of us there is a Source of strength, knowledge, and wisdom. With faith, we can reach out to the unknown and trust and test these resources.

You never know what you have going for you and in you until you test yourself. In fact, I believe that a sensible, courageous attitude toward risk-taking may even be good for your health, since boredom can be fatal. Of course there is some stress involved in taking risks, but the stress itself doesn't make the difference. It's your attitude toward it that counts. In fact, stressful events can be a good thing for some people. They can lead to real growth. Anyone who is accustomed to the rewards and uncertainties of taking risks could tell you this.

If a bold, dynamic approach to life can be beneficial to your health, it only stands to reason that the riskless rut, where nothing is ventured or gained, can be equally as bad. I have always felt a certain sense of closure in my life, when restlessness infiltrated my existence. I have learned to recognize this as a signal for a new beginning, a new change or opportunity to stretch my comfort zones. This closure is typified by restlessness, boredom, and a certain dullness about life.

I recognize it now as a time to become aware of and open to new opportunities. The risks always came when I did not know where those new doors were located, where they opened to, or what they were.

It seems necessary that we close before we risk. Then we are free to put all our energies into the future, rather than in hanging on to the past. The readiness is there. However, a new door opens only when we're truly ready.

This phenomenon is likened to an electronic door. It opens just as you are ready to go through it. All the doors I have tried to force open in my life were wrong for me and my forced efforts had the potential to cause great pain. I've learned a lot, though, from crashing into and through doors!

Ready, Set, Go

When you learn to wait for this readiness and timing, there is a certain inner confidence that you take forward with you, even though outer circumstances might contradict it. You move into the unknown with an inner knowledge that it's the right thing for you to do. I have always trusted this inner knowledge. It frequently comes through intuition. Sometimes it takes courage to follow our intuition, because before we are willing to stretch we are conditioned to look for outside evidence and support for our decisions.

I remember this inner feeling of knowing it was right for me. I remember the peace I felt within myself when, with three small children, I drove away from my hometown at the end of a marriage and headed down the road to begin college.

All of the external circumstances and support systems I was comfortable with no longer existed for me. As I sat behind the wheel of that car, with minimal possessions and many responsibilities, I experienced a sense of confidence, peace and rightness about my decision to stretch. Nothing around me supported these feelings. In fact, my circumstances told me I should not feel such confidence at all.

Those moments have remained a point of reference for the rest of my journey. I often check back on that inner feeling when my inner voice says "right" and everything else says "wrong." This knowingness has been the checkpoint for other major life changes.

First and foremost, I feel in my body that the time is coming. Then I wait for the sense of readiness and rightness to point me in the direction of my newest risk.

One Step Forward, Two Steps Back

It appears that there are always potential losses involved with every risk. These losses, to name a few, include losing someone's love and approval, losing control, or losing face.

I have talked with many clients who feared furthering their education or accepting a promotion or increase in salary because they feared upsetting the balance in a significant relationship.

Joan was a budding success as a salesperson. Since her income was based on a commission, the only factor limiting her financial success was her own choice of energy and time. But curiously, she reached a plateau in sales and didn't progress beyond it.

This situation puzzled her superiors. Eventually, the real issue came out into the open. What held her back was her fear of out-producing her husband financially. At home, she was beginning to hear comments from her husband. "You won't need me any more." "You can support yourself." "I'll be known as the 'superstar's husband'." Joan weighed the potential loss of this relationship against her financial success, and backed off from her work productivity.

When situations like this occur, what usually follows is masked resentment. Ultimately though, the anger breaks through and damages the very relationship we're trying to protect.

Oh yes, losing power and control — how frightening! Especially if we place our control in externals. What will happen to us when we give up the reins? Such bondage stops all growth and creativity.

We manipulate in very cunning ways to keep control. Fear of punishment, withholding information, unwillingness to share knowledge, refusal to delegate, rewards, helplessness, sickness: These are some of the ways we manipulate others to maintain the status quo and keep our comfort zones intact.

I remember a school administrator who made the following statement to me: "I only have three years until retirement. I just want to hold on that long." During those three years, I doubt there was much excitement, challenge or creativity going on.

Letting it All Hang Out

Our perception of how others see us, in addition to our perception of ourselves, can positively or negatively motivate us to take risks. When you follow your own true path, it will no doubt ruffle a few feathers and cause tongues to wag. The old adage, "If no one is talking about you, you're probably not doing much" is well said.

"What if I open the business and I don't make it?"

"What if I take the job and it doesn't work out?"

If we so greatly fear the perceptions of others, we could go on and on for years, never risking. The choice is either to risk or rot. (Well, at least we would stagnate!)

We were created to expand. Do you really want to remain a freshman at the University of Earth for the rest of your life? Of course not.

But one thing is certain: No single risk will solve all your problems. Don't expect it to. Up ahead are other challenges and opportunities for growth. There are other classrooms, other experiences, other risks, and other victories. They all add up to something called living.

Cool Down

Just as the body has a stress response, it also has a

balancing mechanism to counteract stress. In the best-seller, **The Relaxation Response**[1], Harvard cardiologist Herbert Benson calls this mechanism the "relaxation response." This physiological reflex lowers heart and respiration rates, relaxes muscles, decreases the production of stress hormones, and tranquilizes the mind and emotions.

It's no wonder that people who regularly practice a relaxation technique are less anxious and tense. They are better able to resist stress. These people also report feeling happier, more optimistic, self-confident, energetic, and productive. Research has also demonstrated that the relaxation response counteracts the cumulative impact of stress on your health.

Unfortunately, the stress response occurs automatically. But as Dr. Benson points out, the relaxation response must be consciously and purposefully evoked. Lounging about on your massage recliner just won't do it! To elicit the relaxation response, you've got to get into an altered state of consciousness. This may sound mystical. But as Dr. Benson explains: "An altered state merely refers to a level of consciousness that we don't ordinarily experience."

If you've ever slipped into a trance-like state of wakefulness while looking out a window or driving on a monotonous stretch of highway, you've already experienced altered consciousness. The relaxation response is called upon at another level, one that doesn't usually occur spontaneously. It is described by researchers as "a state of profound rest and heightened awareness."

Transcendental meditation, Zen and Yoga, deep breathing, visualization or guided imagery, autogenic training, progressive relaxation, and hypnosis: These are just a few of the techniques implemented to achieve total relaxation. Peaceful sounds, calming colors, soft lighting, comfortable furniture, simple surroundings, a pleasant vista, and freedom from interruption: These are great aids to relaxation. Many of us live in high gear and our primary health need is often just to relax so we can restore our vitality.

Laugh...It's Great Medicine

Norman Cousins, in his book **Anatomy of an Illness**[2], presents the most famous case of using humor to heal. The core of his message relates how negative emotions harm the body and how positive emotions release beneficial chemical reactions.

He described healing himself of a crippling, life-threatening disease by watching videotapes of a favorite comedian and taking massive doses of vitamin C. Based on his systematic use of humor to improve his body chemistry, Cousins reported that ten minutes of "belly laughter" produced a pain-killing effect that lasted for at least two hours.

One possible explanation for the pain-relieving effects of hearty laughter is that laughter increases levels of endorphins and enkephalins in the brain. These substances act as the body's natural opiates. Empirical research shows that when a person finds something amusing, there is an increase of a certain antibody which fights disease. Other effects of laughter include greater respiratory and muscular activity, oxygen exchange efficiency, and decreased heart rates. Perhaps people who don't jog for exercise can get many of the same benefits by including lots of laughter in their lives.

There is some evidence, also, that smiling is beneficial. It takes fewer muscles, we've been told, to smile than to frown. Smiling also induces better feelings when we are anxious or depressed. Smiling is something we could all do more of. It's easy and it's natural. It might even become a habit!

Keep on Keepin' On

Your desire to keep going is the most important thing. If you aren't determined to make the best of an illness, the miracle drugs and treatments of a doctor still won't improve your condition. Our health is influenced by our feelings of self-determination, control, accomplishment and freedom of expression.

What better arena than our immediate surroundings for developing these feelings? Self-determination can mean an action as small as opening or closing a window as we desire. Or it can mean conceiving of and executing a remodeling job. To take responsibility for your environment is to combat feelings of helplessness. Any way you maintain, adjust, or improve your environment in nurturing ways increases your sense of importance and competence.

Whenever you imagine and carry out an environmental improvement plan, no matter how small, you achieve a physical result as well as enduring evidence of your ability to change your world for the better. Any time you put something of yourself into your environment, you give yourself a lasting gift. Such care increases feelings of self-love. It encourages us to be more giving with others. We often act and view ourselves as victims of our environments and circumstances. We do little to improve those circumstances, however.

Knowing When to Move

It's important that we distinguish between what we **can** and **cannot** control. But when life feels out of control, you can regain a grip by taking on a new challenge. Only take action on those problems that you can control. It is necessary that we assess the importance of each of these situations and determine how much energy we wish to expend on any particular problem.

Sometimes we have no choice. Emergency situations present themselves and we must act immediately. All other priorities suddenly slip down a notch or two as we react. How many times have we worked ourselves into a frenzy over something that was of very little value or consequence?

Before you start pumping energy into a situation, ask yourself how important it is to you personally. Can you really make a difference? What's the worst possible outcome if you don't get involved? Getting involved with our own health — spiritual, physical, mental, and emotional — should be our top priority.

Knowing When to Stop

Often through illnesses we rediscover the meaning and

purpose of our lives. There are many people who are sick and have lost sight of the meaning of their lives. Illness can, however, have positive outcomes. We learn an invaluable lesson by looking at the way Eastern cultures view illness. To these cultures, an illness is not necessarily a disaster (previous chapter) or crisis. Rather, it is an event that can represent the beginning of a whole new way of seeing or experiencing life.

In the Eastern philosophies, an event is not judged as good or bad. It is just an event. How it influences your life over time determines whether it's good or bad. Something may strike you as being very fortunate when it occurs. But five years down the road, you may wish it had never happened, because of what it led to.

On the other hand, it may seem that something tragic has happened to you. But in the long run, you may find the event enriched your life. The body may be less, but the total person is more. Sometimes there is more to having an illness than returning to a pre-illness state.

Human nature moves forward with every experience, positive or negative. Something as important as a major illness can really catapult you ahead, mentally, spiritually, and emotionally. Sometimes our bodies stop us so we can take time for reflection and re-evaluation. This "time out" is a gift of time which allows us to re-evaluate, renew, and reinvest ourselves in life.

The Key — Belief and/or Faith

Perhaps you're familiar with the placebo effect where a

harmless, sugar-coated pill cures a headache. The individual who took the harmless pill was told the pill would cure him. Someone this individual trusted and respected claimed the pill was a new-fangled, high-powered drug. The headache sufferer believed it would work, so it did.

Even in those instances when we take a medication with its own specific effects, the placebo effect may still occur. We take it on faith that it will work, so it does.

Just the presence of a well-respected doctor can have the same effect. Before the discovery of antibiotics and all of our scientific technologies, patients still were healed through such practices as folk medicine, mustard poultices, and doctors' suggestions that were received without critical thought. All of these practices and suggestions were trusted.

A placebo gives people permission to heal themselves through the strength of their own beliefs. What is new and promising today is the recognition that the placebo effect can occur without a pill or potion and requires no deception to produce improved well-being. The main ingredient is the human belief system.

Bernie Siegel, the physician who wrote the best-seller *Love, Medicine and Miracles*[3], is teaching those whom he calls "exceptional career patients" to use their inner healing capabilities while continuing to take advantage of conventional methods to treat cancer. Dr. Simonton, of Texas, and other physicians and psychologists are teaching patients to use mental imagery. Mental imagery helps the immune systems of these patients defeat malignant cancer cells. These health care professionals and others emphasize the mind/body connection. They believe it is the body that heals, not the physician.

It is a belief in medication, God, diet, and doctor that mobilizes our inner healer. The greatest key to turning on the inner healer is to accept ownership of your life. If we take charge and believe that we're in charge, we will be.

The human body is its own pharmacy, successfully filling its own prescriptions. The greatest news is that we have the power to rewrite the programs and prescriptions for our own bodies.

(1) Herbert Benson, **The Relaxation Response** (William Morrow & Company)

(2) Norman Cousins, **Anatomy of an Illness** (1976)

(3) Bernie Siegel, **Love, Medicine and Miracles** (New York, Harper and Row, 1986)

Chapter Six

What Are You Living For?

If one advances confidently in the direction of his dreams, and endeavors to live the life which he has imagined, he will meet with a success unexpected in common hours.

Henry David Thoreau

How would you answer the following questions? What is your life's mission? Do you have a sense of purpose in your life? It may be that you have never really considered these questions. It may be that you have considered the questions for someone else, but what about you? What is the goal or objective of your life? Where are you headed? How far along are you? How are you going to get to where you're going? What motivates you? What are you trying to achieve? Have you defined your life's mission?

Mission: Possible

All of us define our mission in some way. Some of us realize we have; some do not. Some say they live purely for pleasure. Others live to prosper, because prosperity gives them a sense of security, and they like security. Some might say: "Well, as I look at my goals and objectives, I live for prestige and status. I like the acceptance. I like the recognition." Others admit they live for power. They like to be in control.

So, all of us live for something. What is it? Ponder this question in your heart: "What are you really living for?"

All of our actions and our attitudes point to what we are living for, where we are headed and what it is we want to accomplish or achieve in life. Some people float through life. They have no goals and no real objectives, no sense of direction, and no mission.

They live from one day to the next, from one week to another and on to the next month. The goal of these people is primarily to squeeze pleasure and contentment from each moment of their lives. They have, however, no real sense of purpose. Their self-centered lives are devoted to doing whatever is necessary, whenever, and wherever in order to please themselves.

The self-centered person is basically insensitive to the needs of others, because he or she focuses on himself or herself. All of this is very subtle. You may not realize until now that your life is centered on yourself, your desires, your needs, and your concerns.

Self-examination will probably help you to sort the whole thing out. The self-centered person lives a life that is empty. It has no genuine contentment and no real joy.

To experience true joy and contentment, one must live a life of giving. The self-centered person directs most of his energy to receiving and misses out on the opportunity for contentment. That's why it's important to reverse the flow of expectation for yourself to one of the joy of giving of yourself to others.

Mission Statement

"Mission" is a word that the corporate world is familiar with. There is, most likely, no organization in existence that did not arise from a single idea which led to its mission statement. To me, a mission is essential. Once a mission is established, then the goals follow readily.

What is a mission? I define it as an expression of beliefs. It's doing what you feel is right to do for you. It provides a sense of completeness while fulfilling it. I experience moments of this completeness when I have been giving a seminar, feeling at one with my audience and doing what I personally believe is my vehicle for touching the lives of others.

I have always felt sad for individuals who never had this sense of "oneness" and labor at something that has no meaning for them. A mission is a statement of what a person feels he **must** do. When values and actions are in harmony, we say the person is "mission oriented."

A person with a mission is never at a loss to know what is worth doing. Sometimes this mission removes the individual from the mainstream of life and aligns him or her with a cause that must be dealt with. For this person, there is a compelling sense of rightness about whatever it is he or she is aligned with. Once the mission is defined, it carries us on in the face of defeat, because we **know** the end is worth the struggle.

I have also come to realize that most missions in some way are a service to others. They make the lives of others better. I believe a true mission must be "other-directed" rather than completely self-directed. What follows, then, are the goals.

Fulfilling the Mission

We should have goals for every area of our lives: personal, family, vocational, and social. A life without goals lacks excitement and tends to drift aimlessly. The individual who has no goals is often critical of those who are achieving. He or she is wasteful, satisfied with mediocrity, and proves to be a disappointment.

On the other hand, a goal-oriented person lives a life that is energetic, enthusiastic, exciting, and expectant. The goal-oriented person is going somewhere and has a plan for getting there. Every great achievement in life begins with a desire. The desire ultimately evolves into a goal toward which the person directs his God-given resources until that goal is reached.

Setting the Goals

It requires more than simple desire, however. The greater the goal, the greater the demands for its attainment. Consider the following as steps for achieving your goals:

1. Formulate a **clear mental picture** of your goal. Remember the power of visualization and see yourself with that goal completed.

2. Feel a **sense of confidence** that your goal can be reached. Remember your inheritance, your pound of worth. It entitles you to pursue anything your mind conceives and believes.

3. Experience a **consuming desire** to achieve your goal. Without passion, there is little promise that your goal will be reached.

4. Develop a **course of action** for reaching your goal. Leave plenty of room for modifying your plan. If your plan is too tightly defined, it's like putting

blinders on. You run the risk of missing opportunities that might further your goals or even change your direction.

5. Find the **courage to act**. Sometimes we might have a wonderful mission and a well-defined course of action. But we fail to consider the courage required for us to act on it.

6. **Persist** in your efforts. Try not to allow external appearances to influence you or lead you to conclude that you will never reach your goal. Faith, belief, and persistence ultimately pay off in the realization of your desire. It's easy to be deceived and sidetracked when your goal is not immediately achieved.

7. Attempt to **control your emotions**. Remember the challenge of learning to manage your emotions, because it's easy to become too emotionally involved. When this happens, we try to take charge and make things happen. The result could become too ego related. It could cause you to lose sight of your mission.

Mission Accomplished...Goals Unmet

You may recall the story of a young man by the name of Terry Fox. A few years ago, this young Canadian was stricken with cancer and sacrificed a leg in his fight with the disease. But Terry was a determined individual. He was driven to find meaning in and a purpose for his life.

His mission was to walk across Canada and raise money for the Cancer Society. He desired this so that others might be helped. He accomplished a portion of that mission, but was unable to complete his walk due to failing health. While his goal was not fully achieved, no one denied that he did accomplish his mission, a selfless mission for the greater good of others.

A Rhyme for All Time

Life, in all its complexities, is often given to us in the simplest of forms. Had we paid more attention to the early nursery rhymes that accompanied our growing up years, we might have had a glimpse of life and how to live it without the pain and struggle associated with trying to figure it out.

"Row, Row, Row Your Boat" is one of the most relevant and pertinent rhymes that comes to mind. Its lyrics follow:

> Row, row, row your boat,
> Gently down the stream.
> Merrily, merrily, merrily, merrily,
> Life is but a dream.

The implications of this rhyme on life have just recently dawned on me. Within its simple phrases, there are great insights that warrant our review.

Row, Row, Row

Where are you going? Hopefully this question has been defined by your mission and your goals. The words "Row, row, row" don't suggest that you row once and then give up. The line encourages you to keep on rowing even when the winds of adversity blow against the little boat of your life.

Eventually, everyone feels the weight of a severe trial, hardship, misfortune, or setback. You find yourself in an unplanned and unanticipated situation. Why did it happen? You were not prepared. Who is to blame?

The key to overcoming adversity is to give the proper response. Depending on your reaction, you can advance beyond the adversity or you can be destroyed by it. The choice is yours. These difficult times, when we are tempted to cease rowing, have hidden within them the potential for increased knowledge.

1. **Adversity** gets our attention. It enables us to re-evaluate the priorities in our lives. It may be a signal that these priorities need to be changed or that a time for self-evaluation is long overdue.

2. **Adversity** reminds us of our real mission. It often protects us from the complete destruction that can result from a self-centered existence.

3. **Adversity** helps us conquer the pride of our egos. Success often breeds pride which, in turn, can lead to failure. Adversity cleanses us and strips away that ego-pride. It leaves us free to realize our true mission.

4. **Adversity** reminds us of those areas in our lives that need work. It clarifies those parts of us that need to grow and stretch. When our backs are to the wall and there seems no way out, we may suddenly realize that we are not sufficient unto ourselves.

5. **Adversity** prepares us to comfort others. We often become more useful to others because of adverse circumstances. We can better empathize with and have compassion for those who are suffering. Perhaps we need to view our trials as a profitable training period which equips us for improved service to others.

Just Keep on Rowing

The following poem, by Charles Osgood, best illustrates this need to persevere.

Hanging in There

If at first you don't succeed, the saying says that then
The thing to do is not give up but try, try again.

But if at first you don't succeed,
A saying isn't what you need.
What you need are some reasons why
It might be worth your while to try.
And now, my friends, would you believe,
I've got a few right up my sleeve.

You say you didn't get the job? You didn't make the
  sale?
Your book has been rejected, and it's thumbs-down
  now, you fail?
Well, before you throw the towel in, before you call it
  quits,
Consider these examples while you're down there in
  the pits:

Lust for Life by Irving Stone, the story of Van Gogh,
Was turned down by many publishers — seventeen
  said no.
The public wouldn't buy this book, Irving Stone was
  told.
At last report now, twenty-five million copies have
  been sold.
And Vincent knew the bitter sting of mean rejection's
  knife.
Of paintings, he sold only one—one painting all his life.
And Julia Child's first cookbook, she would be the first
  to say,
Was rejected, failed as flat-out as a novice's souffle.

Dr. Seuss, the brilliant writer that the kiddies just adore,

Has lots of his rejection slips. Well, maybe twenty-four.
"The Muppet Show" is popular, with its funny, clever
 scenes.
But for twenty years the network couldn't see the show
 for beans.
Beethoven's "Fidelio" was a miserable flop.
It was after the composer died that it came out on top.
And the emperor for whom Wolfgang Amadeus Mozart
 wrote
Criticized one of his operas; said it had too many notes.

Many great composers who are honored so today —
Berlioz and Franck and Shostakovich and Bizet —
Had to cope with great refection, had to do the best they
 could,
Even though some critics said their music simply wasn't
 any good.
The Beatles were rejected, and it seemed they might be
 through,
Before Parlaphone took them on in 1962.
"A balding, skinny actor" — it's in black and white right
 there —
"Can dance little," says the sheet, rejecting Fred Astaire.
 The Steelers once rejected a young quarterback (the
 dolts)
So they later had to face him — John Unitas of the Colts.

The inventor, Robert Fulton, had a quite inventive
 dream
Of ships that would be powered not by wind, you see,
 but steam.

"Fulton's Folly," they all called it, it would never leave
    the dock.
And the man who was behind it was, of course, a
    laughingstock.
Chester Carlson went to Kodak; "No, no, no," he heard
    them say
To the process that's referred to as xerography today.
And a young, part-time reporter in 1933,
Who worked for just a buck a day at the old KTUT,
Was told he'd better stick to print, air talent wasn't his.
"Sorry, Walter," he was told, "but that's the way it is."

To fail is not the terrible disaster it may seem,
If you just hang in there long enough and hold on to
    your dream.
To dream, as William Shakespeare wrote, "To dream,
    ah, there's the rub."
And if at first you don't succeed, well, welcome to the
    club.[1]

So, keep on rowing your boat...

Yes, it is "Your Boat"

We'd be doing just great if only we would spend as
much energy rowing our own boat as we spend attempting
to row everybody else's! We can row beside others and be
available to assist them in some way, pulling them along or
whatever. Ultimately, though, we are responsible and

accountable for our own boat.

When we understand that life is a series of experiences and tests, our road becomes much easier to travel. We constantly create our own future through the thoughts we think and the actions we take in the present.

It's foolish to think we can be punished by some outside force. We are not punished for our actions. Rather, we punish ourselves with our actions. Likewise, we are not rewarded for doing good deeds; we reward ourselves by doing good deeds. When you think you are being rewarded or punished, think of yourself as being the rewarder or the punisher.

According to the law of cause and effect, everything we think or do comes back to us in like form. For example, how many parents tell their rebellious children, "Just wait until you have your own children" or "What goes around comes around"? When we realize that freedom of choice is ours, we can't complain that life doesn't seem to be all we want it to be.

After all, nobody is stopping your boat from changing the direction of your thoughts or actions. This law of cause and effect plays no favorites. It decrees that all of us, no matter how rich or powerful, must reap what we sow. Pleasant or unpleasant, we eventually face the consequences of our actions. It matters little, because it works both ways.

The understanding and acceptance of this concept can have a tremendous impact on our lives. As soon as we realize that we are the creator of our own destiny, we automatically have to stop blaming others and harboring resentments. Select only those thoughts and emotions that produce harmony in your life.

Remember, your subconscious mind is like a willing servant. It does not recognize good or evil, any more than the ground beneath us can distinguish between good and bad seeds. Soil merely brings forth what has been planted. Similarly, the subconscious mind brings forth what has been impressed upon it. Your thoughts are responsible.

Yes, we are accountable for our own boat. In some way or form, we are accountable to our friends, our families, and a higher being.

At this point, it doesn't do any good to complain:

"If only my parents programmed my subconscious mind in a different way."

"If only my parents had approved of me."

"If only my fifth grade teacher hadn't told me I couldn't go to college, I wouldn't be in this mess."

There comes a time, every day, when we must answer to these programs. We are all products of our pasts. But if we remain prisoners of these pasts, it's because we choose to do so.

Gently

Popular phrases like "hang loose," "don't sweat the small stuff" (it's all small stuff!), or "just relax" are familiar to all of us. But too often, they become only cliches or intellectual phrases repeated by rote.

We humans are prone to become tense as we scratch, claw and force our way through life. We too often take the oars of our row boat, grit our teeth, and forge ahead. We end up stranded on sandbars in the middle of nowhere. We live in an "instant" society. We want instant success, with the same expediency that we expect instant coffee.

Most of the pain in my life has come from charging ahead and forcing doors open. It becomes necessary, then, to backtrack and pick up the pieces before moving ahead once again. It also becomes necessary to redefine the direction to take.

When You're Ready

My mentor has three words that she often repeats to me: "When you're ready." Just recently, I have begun to realize and internalize the true meaning of these words. I am not the most patient person. For a person like me who makes decisions and takes control of my life, it is often difficult to realize that I really can't "make" life be as I think it should be.

On numerous occasions in the past, the three words "when you're ready" have made me want to hang up the phone in anger. I always think I am ready! After all, I certainly worked hard. I thought it was time for whatever I felt I deserved to occur in my life.

But I have discovered the hard way that everything happens the way it should, if we don't have preconceived ideas about the way it should happen. When you're ready, the "electronically controlled" doors of your life open. They open naturally. Not before or after you need them opened, but just at the right time.

Waiting and preparing for these doors to open does not mean that you passively do nothing or that you take no

223

action toward achieving your goals. It does mean that you stretch and take risks with your life.

Some risk-taking makes your life happier. However, many people today are still reluctant to take risks. Risks introduce the possibility of failure and success. Since people don't like failure, many play it safe and avoid taking chances. Their decision to stay with what they do have is safer than risking it for what they might have.

Down the Stream

Once again, learning to "go with the flow" doesn't mean passively waiting for the winds to blow you somewhere. It doesn't mean that you put no effort or preparation into your journey. Yes, there is a time to just coast and flow. This time comes **after** you have done all you need to do.

Some people interpret "going with the flow" as not requiring any effort on their part. They react to life rather than acting to utilize the currents which will get them where they want to go. Risk-taking is necessary. It can liberate and provide new opportunities for fulfillment and happiness.

That's why it's important to try to break out of unhappy situations and not endure them just because you feel helpless and hopeless. Although your unhappy situation is **known**, and therefore more comfortable than the **unknown**, it's better to take risks in the hope that changes will be for the better.

Taking the first risky step requires that you articulate your dreams and goals. Then, it's necessary to determine if your dream is a realistic one at the present time. Sticking with a dream that never pays off is the same as not risking. When you claim that you could have been this or that if it hadn't been for society, this excuse is merely another way to blame others for your own shortcomings.

Playing it Safe

There are several categories of "safe players":

1. The **lost soul** plays the victim, instead of taking the opportunity to prove himself or herself. The lost soul says, "I can't do it because no one loves me." This person seeks the response, "Oh, yes, we do love you just the way you are."

2. The **fixer** also avoids change by refusing to deal with personal difficulties. Instead, the fixer gets people to like him or her by solving their problems.

3. **Option opters**, who have made life choices, may also avoid making risky decisions.

4. **Seekers** need so much information before making decisions that they usually end up not making any.

5. **Opinion holders** don't risk getting to know others, because they may have to change their opinions. They are also reluctant to take chances.

6. **Cover ups** use humor or a smile to hide their hostility or true feelings. They do not often take advantage of growth opportunities.

Playing it Masked

To act out a role instead of being oneself is a common way to avoid risks. People who aren't risk-takers often play traditional roles. A "tough guy" father or a "loving" mother or wife are common roles chosen as alternatives to being oneself.

Fathers may not always feel like tough guys and mothers may not always feel loving. But people who act out these roles are afraid others will reject them if they show their true colors. In their pursuit of the affection of others, they play roles they feel will assure that they get this affection.

Those with poor or weak self-images will not risk revealing what they think or feel. They often try to please others or to fulfill the imagined expectations of those around them. It's an unhealthy existence. Eventually, they erect barriers between their "real" and "pretend" selves, barriers that become harder and harder to camouflage as they get older.

People often fill their lives with distractions. Rather than coping with their unhappiness, they become connoisseurs of food or travel or they drink or work too much.

Go With The Flow

The situation, however, is not hopeless for those who

don't ordinarily take risks. These people must first become aware that there is something wrong with their lives. Taking appropriate action must then follow this realization. People who don't take risks also need to practice being clear about what they want from life. They also need to be clear about whom they want to please.

Being happy is not always easy. But the odds are in your favor. "Going with the flow," then, is using the tides and currents of life to your advantage. Use them to get the knowledge, experiences, and the preparations for the next leg of your journey. It means doing so without anxiety, fear and all the other defenses we implement to avoid fulfilling our true potential.

Merrily, Merrily, Merrily, Merrily

To react to life in a positive manner means that we must discard the negatives in our lives. Happiness and peace of mind are the goals of almost everybody.

Most people feel they would reach these goals if certain things were added to their lives. "If only I had...," they say. "If only I could do...," they complain. Happiness, though, generally depends on subtracting from your life, rather than adding to it. Happiness depends on discarding, rather than acquiring.

Sorting it Out

We must discard regrets about the past and all the

hidden grudges that we nurse so faithfully. Also to be weeded out are fears for the future and all the false beliefs we have about ourselves.

If something from the past bothers you, face it squarely. You might say: "It was a mistake, but I didn't know any better at the time. I didn't have the knowledge I have now. If the same situation were to arise again, I would react differently."

Don't scold or punish yourself for something that was just another experience in the pattern of your life. If you learn from your experiences, they won't be repeated. You can move on.

You know you embrace worthless concepts about yourself, if you tell yourself such things as, "I'd never be able to do that, because I don't have the talent or the willpower."

... Choose Your Tomorrow Today

If you decide you'd like to change your attitude, try telling yourself:

"There is nothing I can't have or do if I cultivate a strong desire for it and work toward it."

"I have unlimited powers within me."

"All the obstacles that prevented me from achieving my goals are now removed."

Repeat such statements often and with conviction. Thoughts and words have much more power when they have the support of belief and emotion. These positive statements soon become a part of your subconscious and you will automatically begin to think this way.

Remember, when you rid yourself of negative concepts, you create a void with plenty of room for new thoughts. You actually reconstruct your mind by getting rid of all the junk that has accumulated there over the years. The present is the only time that counts! It is what we do today that determines the nature of our future.

Happiness is a Choice

We all want to be merry and happy. However, we don't always **choose** to be happy. Making the choice to be happy might seem ridiculous at first. How can we possibly be happy if we're weak, sick, poor, or afraid?

We can come to understand that happiness is not necessarily glee, exuberance or utter bliss. Happiness is not as much an expression as a context, a launching pad for the attitudes, actions, and reactions that follow.

If we knew that the dreams of our hearts were coming true, wouldn't we be happy in spite of how the present looked? If we knew, beyond a doubt, that our happiness was causing these dreams to come true, wouldn't this be incentive enough for us to be happy?

We've put the cart before the horse in assuming that conditions must be "just so," before we can open up to the enjoyment of life. We tend to defer our happiness until everything falls into place.

. . . It's an Inside Job

Once the inner choice is made for happiness, things

perfectly and wonderfully take care of themselves. Material things can't make us happy. Neither can the love of another person. Love helps. It's the most powerful healing agent known. But it can't do the trick, if we don't let it.

Sometimes, we almost mistake **need** for **love**. Certainly we need other people, but absolutely not for the purpose of making us happy and complete. We are happy and complete already!

Two people locked into a relationship based on need precariously lean on each other like two playing cards. If one moves even a hair, both collapse. When we're deeply happy within ourselves, when we're aware of and celebrating who we are, we draw others into our lives who feel similarly about themselves. Then, we bask in the glow of each other, instead of trying to be the light in each others' darkness.

... Regardless

Sometimes, we have the notion that a problem-free life is a prerequisite for happiness. But who is without problems? Can we even imagine what it would be like to have no challenging occasions to rise to?

I think what we really want is not freedom from problems, but rather freedom from experiencing the same problems again and again. We need to stand back and ask ourselves just what it was we learned from a particular problem situation. Why are we repeating this same class again?

Obviously, we didn't yet learn what we needed to learn

to move on. More often than not, problems are opportunities in disguise. Opportunities to grow as human beings.

Life is but a Dream

Your life is the manifestation of yesterday's dreams. Your dreams of today become your life of tomorrow. Dream big!

Recently, my mentor reminded me of this power when I talked with her on the phone. As I filled her in on some of the things going on in my life, I made a statement regarding what I felt was an accomplishment.

Her response to my crowing led me to say, "You just let the air out of my balloon." She countered and said, "Then you need to get a bigger balloon." This jolted me into realizing that my dream was so small that even an outside opinion could crush it.

Expect the Best

Parables, while seemingly simple, often teach us great lessons and wisdom. Not only are they used to teach Biblical concepts, but they are also used to illustrate certain life situations. Elie Wiesel includes the following parable in his book **Somewhere a Master**[2].

One day the Czar, while inspecting his troops at the front, fails to notice an enemy soldier whose rifle is aimed at him. Fortunately for the Czar, one of his loyal soldiers pulls the imperial horse's reins and so averts tragedy. The grateful Czar says to his savior, "Tell me your secret wish and consider it granted."

"Majesty," says the soldier, "my corporal is cruel; send him to another company."

"Fool!" the Czar cries out. "Why don't you ask to be made corporal yourself?"

Mr. Wiesel, commenting on this parable, writes:

"Man's tragedy lies not in what he is denied, but in his inability to formulate his desire. He demands too little. He is afraid to set his sight too high. His dreams drag in the dust and his words are empty."

People are afraid to expect too much from life. Their hopes may be dashed. However, we shouldn't allow life's inevitable disappointments to discourage us from pursuing our goals.

The late Rabbi Joseph Luchstein wrote, "What we think of ourselves will determine what we will make of ourselves." The poet Robert Browning understood this when he observed, "Ah, but a man's reach should exceed his grasp, or what's a heaven for?"

Thinkers have, throughout history and through various literary forms, tried to encourage us to be more than we are. The most powerful four words a person can utter are "I think I can." The following rhymed quatrain by Walter D. Wintle summarizes the message well:

Life's battles don't always go
    To the stronger or faster man;
But sooner or later the man who
    Wins is the one who thinks he can.[3]

More From Mother Goose

Once upon a time, the gracefulness and beauty of the seagull came to represent mankind's search for freedom and individuality. On its solitary flight through the heavens, the gull exulted in its freedom. It soared higher and higher, climbing with powerful strokes and coasting downward in majestic swoops and circles.

The "I" of the Seagull

Observations of this same inspiring bird in a group of its own kind depressed and demoralized the observer. The regal seagull, having no sense of fair play or sharing, was often seen attacking other gulls. Even in the midst of its majestic flights, the seagull could be guilty of frenzied and ferocious attacks on other gulls, all for the sake of a small bit of food. So fiercely competitive and jealous are these much idealized birds that, if any one gull is specially marked or set apart in any way, its feathered friends become the instruments of the bird's execution. None of these rejected birds live happily ever after.

"We" are Not Alone!

If mankind selects a feathered symbol representative of his society, we might be better served by the lowly goose. (I know, "loose as a goose" and "silly as a goose" came immediately to my mind, too!) I know "we geese" lack a certain gracefulness and beauty on the ground. But I would like to say a few words on our behalf. Much maligned throughout history, there are several facts, not commonly aired, that prove the aptness of such a selection.

You've long known about and been able to recognize a flock of migrating geese by our "V" flight formation. (By the way, this formation improves our flight speed and efficiency by more than seventy percent!) The lead position of the "V," obviously the most strenuous and difficult, is maintained for only short periods of time. Each vigorous and healthy goose takes its turn at the lead position. This allows all geese to lead and all to fall back to less taxing positions. What a concept!

Additionally, the young, the old, the frail, or the injured birds among us bring up the rear. This enables these birds to make their way where they otherwise might fail. In the event that an individual goose is injured or unable to continue the flight, it is never abandoned; another of the flock stays grounded with the goose until it is once again able to resume the course.

Our annoying "honk" — the sound so often associated with geese in flight — has even been interpreted by scientists as an encouragement for the straggling few! And I personally know many geese who have lived happily ever after!

Free to be "I" and "We"

While I would be among the last to say that a search for expression and individuality is a bad thing, I would lead the flock in saying there is a place for both "I" and "we" in this big world. It matters little if we speak of home, school, or work place. There are times to soar in solo flight and times to pull together into a group. The solitary panting, the grasping for breath and a foothold in this life seem an awfully high price to pay for individuality. You might as easily be part of a group that allows you freedom to lead and a chance to rest!

Both "Row, Row, Row Your Boat" and "More From Mother Goose" illustrate the "I" and "we" of life. If we manage the "I" properly, we have more to give to the "we." The "we" is really our mission in life: to give, to serve, to love others. It can only be done to the extent that we understand and love ourselves.

The End and the Beginning

The End! For some experiences we face, "The end" is an encouraging phrase. For those enjoyable and fulfilling times, it may bring on sadness. But life is filled with endings and beginnings. There is never a true ending. At the end of everything there is the beginning of something new.

The end of every day marks the beginning of
      another.

The end of each experience finds a step that leads to the next new experience.

The end of sickness is health.

The end of labor is rest.

The end of need is sufficiency.

Life has no real finality, just endings and beginnings. Many people drag their yesterdays along behind them. They find that the beauty and opportunities of the present are marred by the haunting specter of their pasts. Leave yesterday where it belongs...on the other side of night. Live your life to its fullest today.

Surely you are familiar with the story of Mr. Jones. He died last night. Yes, he did. He was the wealthiest man in town. Do you know how much money he left behind? All of it.

Though this might be true for many of us, we are still surprised when reminded that we can't take it with us. Not that we expected to, but we're just surprised.

Make More Than a Living...Make a Life

These days, we too often judge the success of a person's life by the trappings associated with making a successful living. In actuality, the two have little to do with each other. Okay, okay! I'll grant you that material comfort is probably a goal common to all of us. But it's a goal too often distorted and carried to an extreme.

What you earn or are given is what determines your **living**. That which you give away is what determines your **life**.

A Christmas Carol Revisited

Those who enjoy the best in life are not necessarily the ones who work the hardest. Those who have the least materially are not necessarily the ones who are the most unhappy.

Each year, for instance, we are reintroduced to Ebenezer Scrooge and Bob Cratchit. While these characters only exist as fictional creations, both typify this concept. While slaving for years in the employ of Mr. Scrooge, Bob received little in the way of material compensation. He was, however, a happy man. Ebenezer did very little in the way of actual work. He had much to call his own, but he was a miserable human being!

Now, where do you see yourself along this continuum of effort, success and happiness?

The Miser Within

This philosophy is more than a suggestion that we stop to smell the roses. It encourages us to give away something of ourselves. It matters little if we give of our money, our talents, or our time.

"You can't take it with you."

"It won't keep you warm."

These and other catchy sayings we associate with miserly behaviors refer to any of the three commodities we tend to horde and stockpile.

Every so often, something happens in our lives that reinforces our resolve to become more personally involved in our homes, communities, and professional lives. A family crisis, a neighborhood issue, or an employment problem: each of these might renew our zeal for involvement, change, or motivation. Within days, however, we are back to our single-minded pursuit of success as defined by the majority of our society.

RIP — An Epitaph for All Time

I often ask myself: "What do I want to be remembered for? Who do I wish to be remembered by?" Much of what I spend my resources on — whether financial, time, or talent — is admittedly for physical survival. The percentage of myself that I give away is for the survival of my soul, that part of me which hopes to make a difference or to matter in some larger sense. Since I can't take it with me and it won't keep me warm, I want to pass on a legacy of a life successfully lived and given away. Poor Mr. Jones. He missed the boat, didn't he?

The question also arises of what goes with us after we graduate from the University of Earth and then advance to new learning experiences. Two things go with us, I believe: knowledge and love. Perhaps that's why our little rowboats aren't very big. We'd only try to fill them with things

238

we didn't really need.

All the learning in the courses we take on our journey better prepares us for the classroom at the next level of existence.

The more we learn, the more we have to share and the better able we are to love. Perhaps the journey is best summarized as loving God first and loving your neighbors as yourself. This is the one Truth discovered on our journey!

(1) Charles Osgood, "Hanging in There," There is Nothing I Wouldn't Do If You Would Be My POSSLQ (Person of Opposite Sex Sharing Living Quarters), (New York: Henry Holt, Inc., 1981), p. 27-28.

(2) Elie Wiesel, Somewhere a Master: Further Hasidic Portraits and Legends (New York: Summit Books, 1982), p. 173.

(3) "The Man Who Thinks He Can," by Walter D. Wintle, from Poems That Live Forever, Selected by Hazel Felleman, Doubleday & Co. Inc., New York, 1965, P-310.

Epilogue

Ships are Meant to Sail

Ships are constructed on land and once put to sea, can never return to the land of their creation.

Ships come in all shapes and sizes. Some ships are christened amid great fanfare and celebration, while others set sail with scarcely a ripple.

All ships have one purpose, and this is to carry and to serve their masters in some way.

Some ships begin their journeys with elaborate and detailed plans to follow. Others merely drift into distant ports.

Some ships never leave the safety of a harbor. They play it safe because they fear the tides and currents of the sea. Others set forth with much determination and a well-defined mission to fulfill.

Few ships complete their missions without weathering storms, high tides, or rough waters. It is at these times that the endurance of a ship is truly tested. Perhaps even more devastating for a tightly-planned journey are those times of absolute calm and little movement.

Some ships arrive at their ports to find others awaiting their arrival. The cargo they carry is in great need.

The cargo capacity for most ships is determined largely by the size and seaworthiness of the ship. If a ship loads too much cargo, it risks sinking. On the other hand, should a ship load too little, it is likely the journey will prove wasteful and counterproductive.

Some ships try to enter chosen ports only to discover the harbor is full. The fullness of a harbor has nothing to do with the adequacy of the ship's cargo. The timing is just off a bit and it's time to sail on.

Ships tied too tightly in the harbor are destined to be broken apart. As the waters lash out against them, they are dashed against each other and their moorings. They are doomed to be destroyed. Any ship tied too tightly is crushed by the fury of the sea, for ships were meant to sail.

Some ships end up marooned on sandbars or on coral reefs. Then it becomes necessary to await repairs and the rising of tides to release them from their prisons.

Some ships must return to port to have barnacles scraped from their hulls. Although it may appear that nothing is going on during these times, the cleansing is a preparation to sail again.

Some ships sail in groups, only to find that cross currents separate them. Each ship, then, is pulled off in a new and different direction.

Ships lost at sea will forever be a part of the sea.

Ships not properly cared for may spring leaks or suffer structural damage. Such damage may lead to the ships sinking or being dry-docked for expensive, time-consuming repairs which make them seaworthy again.

When the journey is completed and the mission is fulfilled, the ships leave harbor for the last time. As they fade into the sunset, tearful crowds disappear behind them.

As these ships round the bend and enter the next cove, they are greeted by other groups awaiting their arrival. With smiles and outstretched arms, the crowds welcome the newly-arrived ships.

There is no ending, just a continuation of the journey.

For ships were meant to sail.

Sail on!

DR. CHARLENE BELL, Ed. D
Educator, Psychologist, Consultant

Now you can share
Dr. Charlene Bell's message
with friends and associates

Dr. Charlene Bell, known internationally for her unforgetable down-to-earth presentations, inspires her listeners with real solutions to everyday problems.

Most important . . . Dr. Bell is available to provide her exciting solutions as a speaker for your workplace training, organization meeting or convention.

* * *

"Her programs succeed in getting people to turn theory into practice. Her approach really works."
Pioneer Hi-Bred International, Inc.

* * *

Dr. Bell's reputation as a persuasive and dynamic speaker has spread throughout the business community.

Clients enjoying Dr. Bell's expertise include:

Meredith Corp.
Principal Financial Group
Hawkeye Bank Corp.
John Deere
National Pork Producers
Diet Centers
Hospice Organizations

American Mutual Life
Farm Bureau
NW Bell Telephone Co.
American Red Cross
State Colleges and Universities
Human Resource Associations
More than 50 hospital staffs

Independent Small Business Employers

244

"A positive difference in the way individuals interact with each other is already apparent."

Methodist Medical

Dr. Bell combines her experience as a psychologist and educator to create innovative and animated presentations that stimulate groups of any size. She will also work with you to design a program that meets your specific needs.

Her most popular programs are:

THE JOY OF CHANGE — A realistic approach to making dynamic improvements in your life, both personally and professionally.

A COMPANY CALLED YOU — A dynamic experience in lifestyle, stress and self-management.

PROBLEMS, PREDICAMENTS AND LOST CAUSES — A practical approach to solving the common, but troublesome, situations which affect us all.

WHEN YOU TALK TO YOURSELF LISTEN CAREFULLY — Vital insight into healthy self talk to optimize your outlook, focus your plans and keep you on top, in touch and going for it.

For more information on how you can schedule Dr. Charlene Bell for your next convention, professional gathering or workplace training, simply call 1-800-728-3187.

A speaker's portfolio with additional details will be sent to you immediately.